THE NATURE OF MYSTICISM

IS VOLUME

38

OF THE

Twentieth Century Encyclopedia of Catholicism

UNDER SECTION

IV

THE MEANS OF REDEMPTION

IT IS ALSO THE

138TH

VOLUME IN ORDER OF PUBLICATION

Edited by **HENRI DANIEL-ROPS** *of the Académie Française*

THE NATURE OF
MYSTICISM

By M. D. KNOWLES

HAWTHORN BOOKS · PUBLISHERS · *New York*

248.8
K

First Edition, October, 1966

NIHIL OBSTAT

Joannes M. T. Barton, S.T.D., L.S.S.

Censor Deputatus

IMPRIMATUR

✠ Patritius Casey

Vicarius Generalis

Westmonasterii, die VII JULII MCMLXVI

The Nihil Obstat and Imprimatur are a declaration that a book or pamphlet is considered to be free from doctrinal or moral error. It is not implied that those who have granted the Nihil Obstat and Imprimatur agree with the contents, opinions, or statements expressed.

9572

CONTENTS

ACKNOWLEDGEMENTS

For the purpose of quotation in this book the following texts have been used:

The Cloud of Unknowing and other Treatises, edited by Dom Justin McCann, London, Burns and Oates, 1924, and Westminster, Md, Newman Press, 1952; *The Scale of Perfection* by Walter Hilton, edited by Dom Gerard Sitwell, London, Burns and Oates, 1953, and Westminster, Md, Newman Press, 1954; *The Complete Works of St John of the Cross*, translated and edited by E. Allison Peers, three volumes, London, Burns and Oates, 1943, and Westminster, Md, Newman Press, 1953; *The Complete Works of St Teresa of Jesus*, translated by E. Allison Peers, London and New York, Sheed and Ward, 1946; *The Spiritual Doctrine of Sister Elizabeth of the Trinity*, translated by a Benedictine of Stanbrook, Westminster, Md, Newman Press, 1947. I wish to thank the translators, editors and publishers concerned for permission to quote from these works.

In the cases of St John and St Teresa I have occasionally, for isolated words and sentences, made use of the old (David Lewis) translation of St John, of the Stanbrook translation of St Teresa, or of my own version of the Spanish, where textual or other reasons made a difference of opinion permissible, but as the present book is intended for the general reader, while these alterations are alternative versions, not critical emendations, I have not cumbered the text with numerous footnote references. In every case, where the works of the Spanish saints are concerned, a reference is given to the Peers translations, as being those most readily accessible.

In the text, capital letters have not been used for pronouns referring to the Deity or to Christ; in quotations, the practice of the text that is used has been followed.

D.K.

CHAPTER I

WHAT IS MYSTICISM?

Everyone in our day who proposes to speak or to write of
mysticism must begin by deploring both the ambiguity of the
word itself and the difficulty of defining it in any of its meanings. Yet without some sort of definition and some kind of
understanding between writer and reader as to what is being
discussed no progress of any kind can be hoped for. Consequently, before attempting to answer the question that forms
the heading to this chapter it will be well to say that in this
book we are primarily concerned with traditional Christian
mysticism. On a later page we shall take a wider view, and
try to decide to what extent, if at all, the various apparently
mystical experiences found outside Christianity and indeed
outside any religious context are in fact identical with or
similar to Christian experience. But for the moment, writing
as Catholic Christians committed by our faith to a belief in
the direct communication between God and the soul of man,
we cannot proceed in any other way than that of defining first
of all what we hold to be the veritable form and end of the
mystical experience in its purest form.

This explanation is necessary because, for historical reasons
which would need a lengthy exposition and which need not
be elaborated here, all general interest in mysticism was absent
both within and without the Catholic Church for some two
centuries before the twentieth. Mystics, hidden and not so
hidden, certainly existed and even wrote of their experiences,
but outside Catholic circles such people were widely regarded

as instances of the abnormal or of the occult, if not as simply hysterical or fraudulent, and within the Church they were left to their spiritual directors and to the small group of theologians interested in such things. A revival of interest began simultaneously towards the end of the nineteenth century in two quarters for different reasons. Outside the Catholic Church the scientific study of psychology, largely in its morbid and abnormal, or at least in its subliminal and pre-rational manifestations, became common. This was conducted primarily by non-believers or those unorthodox by traditional theological standards, and was directed principally towards psychiatry and the establishment of a balanced personality. Its adepts proceeded by way of observation and empirical methods, and were interested in religious phenomena only as providing further instances of unusual psychological conditions. It must be added, that this psychology, though preserving the traditional name of a department of philosophy very closely connected with theology, had an entirely different subject-matter. To the Christian (and, though with wide differences, to many schools of philosophy) the human soul is an entity in its own right, directly created by God to "inform" the body and to make up with it the human being. This soul, of itself a spiritual being, gives actuality to all the powers and faculties of the body, but has also, of itself, intellectual and volitional powers which make it capable of rational knowledge of the universe about it and of freewill to direct its activities and to control and direct its love. Its natural capacities are indeed limited to a knowledge of beings of which it has experience or of which it can by reason and intuition deduce the existence and nature, but the Christian knows that his soul was created "in the likeness of God" in order that it might be raised, by means of what theologians call the potentiality of obedience, to a far higher and more intense knowledge and love, that of God as he is in himself. And as love implies union with its object, and knowledge if adequate implies equality in some degree,

God can be known and loved in himself only by a being to whom he has given something of his own divine nature.

The modern psychologist, as such, has no such wide view. By the psyche he understands simply the active principle that manifests itself in all the cognitive, volitional and emotional movements of the human being. It is not part of his science to assume the data of philosophy or theology, and indeed philosophy, in the world of today, would provide no firm basis of any kind. In consequence, the psychologist can do no more than treat what he hears of mysticism as one among many of the "varieties of religious experience".

While psychology was developing as a science by observation, Catholic thinkers, for the most part not expert in technical theology, were reacting against the prevalent arid rationalism and materialism by interesting themselves in the direct, personal experiences and writings of the celebrated mystical saints of the past. Some were drawn by devotional motives, others hoped to use the mystical experience as an argument for the truth of Christian belief, but most of these Catholic thinkers, in this resembling the psychologists, approached the subject from outside, with a quasi-scientific technique of observing and comparing phenomena in the hope of arriving at general conclusions and a definition of their subject. Gradually, and especially in England, mysticism became a subject of study and research, and came to embrace a wide arc of experience as treated by William James, Evelyn Underhill and Baron Friedrich von Hügel. While many of these writers and thinkers were believing Catholics, they made no attempt at a theological analysis of the mystical experience. They might judge mysticism to be a true and valuable "element of religion", and even consider that the experiences of the Catholic mystics were the deepest and most spiritually significant, but they remained on the phenomenal level, amassing and comparing the accounts of the mystics themselves. One result, or it may have been the manifestation, of this new interest was a shift in devotional and even of popular interest towards mystical writings of all ages and countries. Works unpublished or long out of print became, and have remained, popular.

As a result, there was for long no consensus of opinion, even among the best qualified writers on mysticism, as to what precisely mysticism or contemplation might be. One has only to glance at the writings of Abbot Cuthbert Butler, in the editions of the 1920's and 1930's, to see the extent of "theological agnosticism" on the subject even in a scholar long interested in the subject, whose findings and conclusions on the mystics have found acceptance at the highest level of Catholic and non-Catholic scholarship. Such an "agnostic" attitude is naturally even more common among non-Catholics, and is both comprehensible and indeed inevitable among non-believers, to whom mysticism must always remain as something to be treated on the phenomenal level, but it is far from uncommon among Catholics, and the revulsion from systematic, scholastic theology, so prevalent at the present moment, will doubtless help to perpetuate it.

Mysticism, both as a word and as a topic of discussion, is of relatively recent birth, and has developed new shades of meaning in the past fifty years. No English dictionary attains absolute precision in its definition. The Oxford English Dictionary gives, among others, the following entry for "mystic": "One who seeks by contemplation and self-surrender to obtain union with or absorption into the Deity, or who believes in the spiritual apprehension of truths inaccessible to the understanding." And for "mysticism" it gives a corresponding entry: "Belief in the possibility of union with the divine nature by means of ecstatic contemplation; reliance on spiritual intuition as the means of acquiring knowledge of mysteries inaccessible to the understanding." These definitions are certainly faulty both from lack of technical precision and mutual agreement (the former has "truths" where the latter uses "mysteries"), and in their use of words that are either otiose (e.g., "ecstatic") or practically synonymous with the word that is being defined (e.g., "contemplation"), but they indicate well enough two fields in which the word commonly occurs, as also the basic element common to both. The basic element is the inaccessibility to the human understanding of the knowledge acquired or received. The two fields are those in which God and Nature respectively are the dominating objects of attention.

In this book we shall be concerned primarily with theological mysticism or, to use the term consecrated by tradition, "mystical theology", and this may be defined as "an incommunicable and inexpressible knowledge and love of God or of religious truth received in the spirit without precedent effort or reasoning". More loosely used, it may comprehend the normal conditions, accompaniments and side-effects of such knowledge, and a description of the circumstances of its reception, and of the attempts made to receive it and to convey its meaning and effects to others.

It may be said, and with some truth, that such a definition begs the whole question. Granted that mystics assert the inexpressibility and incommunicability of their experiences, it is for others to inquire, to discover and to criticize their nature and value, and therefore it is intellectually misleading, even dishonest, to assume their transcendental, or in theological language their supernatural, origin. To this we can only answer that mystical theology is but a corner of a large field, that of theology in all its branches, and that it is intimately linked with the whole body of Christian revelation. If it were necessary to prove at every point the existence and truth of that revelation before considering any particular consequence of it—let us say, the theology of grace, or of the sacraments—the burden would be intolerable. The definition given above must suffice as an indication of our subject, and no attempt will be made to prove the validity of the mystics' claim. On the other hand, it is part of the purpose of this book to explain

the mystical experience by showing what it has in common
with the theology of grace considered as the principle of the
Christian life. This in its turn can be understood and analysed
only from above, so to say, that is, in the light of the common
and traditional Christian teaching whose authority must be
sought in the teaching of Christ and his apostles. To say this
may surprise many, and will certainly not meet with agreement from those (and nowadays they are many) who are interested in mysticism as psychologists or students of religious
experience, and who regard mysticism either as a purely
subjective activity, or as the outward appearance of powers
rare in themselves or at least normally overlaid by superficial
activity or, finally, as a purely natural contact with a power
or spirit within the framework of the universe. Such disagree-
ment is inevitable if we hold that the true mystical experience
is an instance of the (normally imperceptible) action of God
within the soul and powers of a human being. If we hold this,
any consideration of it must pass, so to say, from God down-
wards before we are in a position to look at the visible evidence and consequences of God's action. God is Spirit; what
is born of the spirit is itself spirit also.

The end of human life, the purpose for which each human
soul was created, is to give glory to God, at the elementary
level by being what God creates it to be, at a higher level
by seeing and acknowledging in thought and action the
sovereignty of God, and at the highest level, itself infinitely
diversified in degree, by loving God as revealed by Christ in
three Persons, Father, Son and Holy Spirit, and by fulfilling
in all ways the will of God as known and loved. The first and
last purpose of human life as seen by Christ is to do the will
of God. To do the will of the Father always, to be and to
remain one with the Father, was Christ's *raison d'être* on
earth, and it is the Christian's also, whether the Father is
seen as one to be feared and obeyed or one to be loved even
to spiritual union. The greatest commandment is to love God

with every power of mind and soul, to show this love by keeping the commandments of Christ, to abide in Christ, and to be perfect as our heavenly Father is perfect. Union with Christ, which he himself compares to the union of his own human soul with the Father or, in other words, the attainment within the limits of a creature of the divine perfection, is the end of human endeavour as seen by Christ. It need scarcely be said that such an end, such an achievement is, to purely human eyes, extravagant to absurdity.

Christ stands alone as one who could claim complete sinlessness and harmony of will with God, and who appears perfect with divine perfection. Such perfection was possible only because his human nature shared in his divinity through his personal and essential union with God. It is only possible, in an infinitely lower degree, to a mere creature through a direct gift of divine powers; one can even say, using the words of Scripture and of the daily liturgy of the Mass, by a sharing of the divine nature.[1] Such a gift, such a consortium, seems the height of extravagance or, alternatively, a meaningless, if not hypocritical or blasphemous, use of words. Yet the words stand, and if we do not acknowledge the power and the love of God which they express, it is because we do not in common life realize even what a likeness of the divine powers we have been given as human beings by our capacity to know and to love. But it is also because we find it hard to acknowledge in thought and word, what we hourly allow in practice, that perfection is of infinitely varying kinds and is reached by a seemingly slow and endless advance. Moral perfection—as indeed also the perfection of art—is not reached as one reaches the terminus of a railway, but as a flower develops from a seed. The flower has already something of its final

[1] "Grant that by this mystery of water and wine, symbols of the human and divine natures of Christ, we may be sharers in the divine nature of him who deigned to share with us in our human nature" (Prayer at the blessing of water at the offertory of the Mass).

beauty as a living creature when the first recognizable green shoot appears. But besides this, we do not find it easy to isolate love, the one thing needful, from all other human qualities and activities, nor do we give a real, as distinct from a notional, assent to the presence and power of sanctifying grace, which by definition is the invisible force which raises the human mind and will to a power beyond anything they could obtain of themselves.

Christ, as we hear and see him in the Gospels, does more than demand our love and obedience for himself and for the Father, he offers and prays for an identity of knowledge and love between the believer and himself. "That they all may be one, as thou, Father, in me and I in thee; that they also may be one in us ... that they may be one, as we also are one; I in them and thou in me; that they may be made perfect in one." [2] These words of Christ, and other similar phrases repeated by St John the Evangelist, have been rightly called "the mystic's charter", but it is surprising how many, indeed how the majority of Christians, can read them without a realization of their mystical force and their stupendous implications. Sometimes consciously, more often unconsciously, the reader regards them as if spoken loosely or in metaphor, not as bearing the full weight of theological sublimity. Christ was speaking for the last time as a man among men, speaking with the clear sight of his redemptive death before him, speaking what was to be a message, a solemn covenant, for all time. He saw his Church, his redeemed, not as defective souls incapable of constancy in their profession of faith in him, but as sons of God who were to be in solidarity with himself, divinely gifted to be members of the Body of which he was Head. We speak of the glory and power of the human reason, clearly visible in a Plato or an Einstein, but even in its lowliest exercise transcending all the material universe. Christ was speaking of the sublimity of the eternal life he gave, recogniz-

[2] John 16. 22–3.

able in a Paul or a John, but existing darkly and in germ in every soul in grace. Supernatural indeed in the smallest act of faith or love, but visibly divine or, more correctly, wholly supernatural and thus transcending all observation, but experienced in the soul itself and radiant by its reflection on the spiritual and material faculties and actions.

The depth of Christ's calling and the practical consequences of his gifts were realized by two or three of those who stood spiritually nearest to him, the apostles Peter, John and Paul. St Peter in his appearances in history in the Gospels and in the Acts seems to have little of the mystic about him. Yet it is he who in one place demands of Christians a holiness defined by the exemplary holiness of God, and in another speaks of Christian souls as sharers or companions of the divine nature.[3] St John the Apostle, for his part, speaks of redeemed souls as truly the children of God who will see him as he is.[4] In St Paul's words, the souls of the just will know God even as they are known by him.[5] The words of SS. Peter and John have been considered, as tradition has always considered them, as the authentic utterances of those who had walked with Christ and heard his words. Even if this were not so, and the words were written by an unknown hand of the second century, they would be, if anything, still more striking, as reflecting the outlook of the early generations of Christianity, an outlook wholly different from that of later Neoplatonic thinkers.

Thus the teaching of Christ, as seen in its presentation by the evangelists and apostles, puts before us a new life, the free gift of God, implying new powers and a new knowledge of God. It is a life lived wholly by virtue of the grace of Christ, without whose agency the Christian can do nothing, and leading to a clear vision of the divine Being. It implies a life of holiness, lived in union with Christ, a union both typified

[3] 1 Peter 1. 15–16.
[4] 1 John 3. 2–3.
[5] 2 Cor. 13. 12.

and fortified by the gift of himself in the holy Eucharist, and based upon the exemplar of God the Father. That the life of the great majority of Christians in every century has borne little resemblance to this ideal should not be a matter for surprise, still less for doubting its reality. Christ himself repeated more than once that many are called but few chosen, and laid down firm conditions for those who would follow him. Those who, by his grace, and by their acceptance of his gifts, have fulfilled those conditions have experienced the truth of his promises.

The term "supernatural" will be used often in these pages. It is a word that is out of favour at the present day. It is indeed meaningless to those who do not acknowledge the existence of a God who has, in a pre-eminent degree, all that we mean by personality and providential care for his creatures whom he loves, and whose love in return he both invites and bestows. Some even of those who profess a belief in a personal, providential God feel an objection to any distinction between his natural and supernatural agency, either because they are unwilling to admit the possibility of any evidence for the supernatural, or because they regard all God's dealings with the universe as something transcendental and not susceptible of analysis and differentiation. All such differentiation and definition must, it is granted, be on our part only. God is absolute simplicity. Creatures have relationship to him, but he has none to them.

Nevertheless, the term "supernatural" is necessary, if only as a symbol, in any Christian theology. Human beings, as such, have certain powers, certain potentialities, and certain modes and conditions of existence. God, on the other hand, and in particular Christ, the Son of God, has bestowed gifts, and made demands and promises, that exceed the exigencies and capabilities of human beings, and the Christian life is directed to an end beyond all human expectations, which can only be attained by powers and actions beyond unaided human capacity. Neither the end, nor the means of attaining it, are visible, save to the eye of faith. Moreover, the means of attaining to the immediate end of the Christian life, the fulfilment of the will of God, are to the outward eye identical, or at least similar, to those which form part of any ethical programme. The life of Christ, to those who lived with him for the first thirty or more years of his existence on earth, was not visibly different from that of an exceptionally good man, and even during his public life those who had no insight regarded him as an ordinary, indeed as a misguided, man. Yet he could claim that those who saw him, saw the Father because, by doing always the will of his Father and seeking nothing but his glory, he was in fact presenting to the world of human beings one like themselves fulfilling exactly all that the Father could wish from a human being who was his Son.

What is strictly "supernatural" is also strictly imperceptible to the normal faculties of man. This is a principle of very great importance in any discussion of Christian mysticism. The natural faculties of man can only perceive the supernatural by its effects. Once they have been given a higher capacity, by the free gift of God that we call grace, they can perceive things above their nature in proportion to the measure of grace they have received, but they cannot express them either to themselves or to others, on the normal level of thought and speech.

CHAPTER II

THE LIFE OF GRACE

Every action of every agent, and above all every action of a free and reasonable human being, is performed with the direct assistance of God, who not only bestows the power to act, but also concurs with the action in such a way that if he withdrew his aid the action would cease. In the case of a natural human action this assistance of God is also natural; it is an integral and necessary condition of his providence for his creation. Despite this assistance the human being is, and is conscious of being, free. How this can be we cannot understand; we can only say that God's omnipotence can bring a free act into being, and note, if we will, that the freedom of the human will is denied the most emphatically by those who do not admit the existence of an omnipotent God.

The purely natural level is not, however, the only level of human action; indeed we may say that it was never, in God's design as revealed to us, intended to be the normal level. The baptized human being, and every other human being who has come to a belief in God and a love of God, is on this higher level. He can perform acts which, either explicitly or implicitly, either actually or virtually, are directed towards God as a loving Father with care for all men, as a Trinity of Three Persons, as a Master, Redeemer and Brother who became man for our sake. For this a higher kind of assistance is indispensable, a free gift which human nature cannot demand or even imagine, the gift named "grace", which is in itself no more perceptible than the natural assistance of God, though it can sometimes be recognized in its effects. This grace, which in its full expansion is the love of God, is a real quality, a real possession of the soul. For its first bestowal it depends upon no previous personal action, it is "infused" in the baptized child before it can be consciously received, and even in the adult coming to God from unbelief it is poured into his soul, and moves his mind and will, at the moment when first he can say, "I believe, Lord". This grace comes, not merely as an impulse to the soul, but as a light and a fire that can grow indefinitely in power and take possession of all the faculties of a man. Theologians speak of the "infused virtues": faith, hope, love; prudence, justice, fortitude and temperance. The division is ancient, part scriptural and part Greek, and our mind, which sees individual actions, must make divisions of one sort or another. But all these acts and powers are aspects of the one great power of God's love poured into our hearts by the Holy Spirit who is Love, through Jesus Christ, the Son and Word of God. The Christian soul grows and approaches to God by receiving and acting with this divine help. As a Christian, and in so far as he is a true Christian, he has new and higher standards than before. Whereas a human being can follow no higher guide than his reason, the Christian must follow the command of God as revealed by his Son, to love God with the whole mind, the whole soul, the whole heart, and one's neighbour as oneself. In other words, the Christian must be united to the will of Christ. The first gift of sanctifying grace gives this love, this union, in their essence and with the possibility of full realization; but they are given as a leaven that must work upon the whole mass, not as a talent to be hidden in the ground. In the words of the poet:

> Our wills are ours, we know not how;
> Our wills are ours, to make them thine.[1]

---

[1] Tennyson, *In Memoriam*, introductory stanzas.

This is not the work of man, but of God, and the Christian's love of God and man, as it grows by practice and effort, is always God's work more than man's, though man makes his own choice and feels that it is his own choice and action. Man feels the effort. "The kingdom of heaven suffers violence." Christ himself felt his human reluctance and fear in the face of the whole sum of spiritual evil in the hour of the power of darkness. The Church bids us pray that God may even "compel our rebellious wills"[2] to turn to him. Gradually, as a soul grows, as in human activities so in this, what was dimly seen and laboriously achieved becomes gradually clear to see and possible (under God) to do. The love of God becomes so much a part of consciousness that the will of God, when seen, is chosen and followed at once. But the assistance of God is as yet given as before, in a human way, as a light and a help to the reason and will, which still have their explicit, perceptible activities.

There is a stage still higher for man's actions. "Those who are moved by the spirit of God, they are the sons of God."[3] The more a soul is conformed to God's will, the more is it susceptible of God's action and help. The clearer a soul's sight, the greater the power of its will, and by an apparent paradox the clearer its sight and the greater its power the more completely does it see with God's sight and act by his power. In other words, the more refined the mind becomes, the more constant and firm the command of the will, the more is the merely human element taken up into the divine control. In yet another way of speaking, the more completely the soul is master of itself, the greater the part of God in the human activity. Theologically speaking, knowledge and love are in greater and greater degree "infused" into the soul, and in purer and purer form, so that while both knowledge and love

---

[2] Secret prayer of fourteenth Sunday after Pentecost: *ad te etiam rebelles compelle propitius voluntates.*

[3] Rom. 8. 14.

are more fully and profoundly experienced, the less is it possible to give them expression in thoughts and words. The soul works less and less by "acts" of "virtues" and more and more by acceptance and submission to the divine impulse. This new and higher form of grace, which is needed by the soul if there are to be no gaps and imperfections in its vision, no slowness and impurity in its will, is an all-pervading light and motion that no longer adapts itself to human ways but raises the human powers to a super-natural level. Christian tradition and medieval theology have given to this grace the name of the Gifts of the Holy Ghost, and tradition has canonized the sevenfold division which is, in a descending order of excellence: wisdom, understanding and knowledge: counsel, piety, fortitude and the fear of the Lord.[4] These Gifts come to the soul at baptism, along with the "theological" virtues and the infused Christian habits of action and, like the other virtues, they enlighten the mind when it is properly disposed. The not uncommon sense of penetrating the meaning of Scripture in accordance with Christian tradition, or of a deeper appreciation of the truths of the faith such as the Divinity of Christ or the absolute sinlessness of the Mother of God, that come to the faithful as well as to the theologian, may be attributed to these Gifts, and such an awareness, when it reaches a certain degree of clarity, is indeed "mystical" for it comes to the mind without discursive reasoning and cannot be communicated fully to others. Nevertheless, the recipient has no kind of mystical "experience", and the light that is received illuminates a truth that is already known and expressed in words, even if the reality of this illumination, as of those of other kinds, is unquestionable and precious.

When, however, the influence of these Gifts is pronounced and habitual, and the soul realizes that the knowledge of God and divine things is of another character altogether from that of past experience, the entrance to the mystical way has taken

[4] Is. 11. 2–3.

place. It is thus that the mystical life, according to constant tradition, is to be attributed to the Gifts of the Holy Spirit. Here again, as with the virtues, a single powerful influence of God on the soul has been broken down into a sevenfold division, based upon a passage in Isaiah and the symbolic force of the number seven. It may well be that the passage in the prophet quoted above, seen in the light of modern critical exegesis, will not bear the weight of theological importance traditionally put upon it, and the same criticism may be made of early patristic references to the Gifts. Nevertheless, the divine influence to which the Gifts have been appropriated is a fact of experience, observed and described by many of the mystics. It is a living spiritual reality, whether we give it the traditional name or attach to it a mathematical symbol, and nothing can be gained by exchanging a name for an x or y, or for a vague general term. The growth of the spiritual life, as set out above, is not an arbitrary or imaginary scheme; it is the life lived by the fervent Christian from the earliest times to the present, shorn of individual details and regarded by the eye of the theologian rather than by that of the mystic.

There is, however, another aspect of the Christian life. It is well to remind ourselves that the Christian mystic has no smooth or gentle passage from strength to strength. The saint, the fervent Christian, is not, when we can see beneath the surface, aiming at the ideal of the pagan philosopher, untroubled by excess or disturbance. Christ promised to his disciples peace, that is, the inmost certainty of faith and trust in God; he also promised a sword and a cross. The call of Christ is not to an easy, humanly reasonable life, but to one lifted upon another plane, on which the golden mean is not the ideal. Hence the dark, and to mundane eyes often distasteful, aspects of the spiritual life, which are still more clearly seen in the mystical life. Besides the normal stresses and sorrows and accidents of life there is the strife and suffering that normally accompany great graces. There is the direct and purifying suffering, bodily, psychological and intellectual, that is the consequence, the obverse side, of divine illumination. The human faculties are not strong enough, the heart and soul not pure enough, to receive the light and love that are filling the soul, and in consequence light appears to be darkness and love is felt as an unbearable deprivation, an unattainable happiness. The excellence of God is unbearable to the imperfect spirit. The mind has to pass from the comfortable world of sense and reason to the simplicity of pure faith, and the way between is cold and dark.

Beyond this, for the true Christian mystic, is the call, made by Christ and answered early by St Paul, to share the redemptive cross, to bear with Christ not only the persecution which is so often the lot of the just man, but also the mysterious burden of evil and sin, which was by far the most severe element in the agony of Christ in the garden and on Calvary. Closely allied to this, and avoided rather than denied by modern minds, is the power of spiritual evil personified, the war of spirit with spirit, which can only take place when the soul is isolated and purified from the material world of sense, and can directly meet spirit both good and evil. It is only when the soul has been purified by the divine action upon it and strengthened by the exercise of faith and love in darkness and in the lack of all feeling, that it is capable of receiving the invisible light of God.

> "Wouldst thou", so the helmsman answered,
>   "Learn the secrets of the sea?
> Only those who brave its dangers,
>   Comprehend its mystery."[5]

[5] Longfellow, *The Galley of Count Arnaldos.*

CHAPTER III

MYSTICISM AND CONTEMPLATION

Hitherto in this book the words contemplation and contemplative have scarcely made their appearance, and readers may have noted this with surprise. The omission was intentional. Mysticism was the title prescribed for the book, and it seemed best to attach a clear meaning to that title before adding further confusion, for contemplation is a term as ambiguous as mysticism. For our present purpose the two words are all but synonymous, and in these pages "contemplation" and "mystical prayer" are interchangeable expressions, but contemplation considered in isolation as a word has a number of other meanings besides its neutral, daily, signification of a prolonged and reflective gaze upon an object of sight or thought. In philosophical language it is the restful penetration by the mind of some truth or proposition reached by a process of dialectical argument or scientific investigation, or, in a somewhat wider scope, the survey by the mind of a whole field of knowledge. This sense of the word, found originally in Plato and used with great frequency and emphasis by Aristotle, became classic as a term of art in ancient and later schools of thought, especially in its adjectival form, and was invariably used in opposition to the words "action" and "active". The contemplation of a truth, or of the whole universe as revealed by observation and thought, was contrasted with the activity of a mind searching for truth or applying its findings to practical ends. The contemplative life was therefore the life of the philosopher gazing at the whole body of known truth for no other purpose than to penetrate its meaning ever more deeply and to rest in a peaceful and enriching apprehension of its inner being and significance. This use of the word was given a more profound and transcendent significance, and an esoteric, almost religious connotation in the system of Plotinus, and passed thence into later Neoplatonic and other schools of thought. It was the highest employment of the mind, to which all study and mental effort tended; it was in itself sufficient and tranquil, but had issue always in a by-product of self-diffusion. From Neoplatonism it passed into the vocabulary of Christian theologians, where it acquired a specifically religious meaning, as the occupation of the theologian penetrating by the aid of grace and revelation into the hidden depths of Christian doctrine. It only remained for it to be used in the vocabulary of the spiritual life of an advanced type of prayer, thus joining the term mysticism at the highest level of their respective meanings.

This history of semantics had a vexatious consequence in all subsequent spiritual literature, for contemplation has been used ever since indiscriminately both for the highest exercise of the mind in penetrating the truths of religion and their meaning, assisted by the Christian powers and graces, and also for the wholly supernatural and infused knowledge of God and of divine things. This confusion, which has existed for more than a thousand years, will doubtless persist in the ages to come, if for no other reason than that the confusion of meaning reflects a profound difference in understanding.

On the one hand, those who do not admit the existence of a personal, transcendent God cannot accept the distinction—the capital distinction—between knowledge acquired by the mind of its own powers, and that infused by God. On the other hand, the everyday writer and reader cannot be at pains to ascertain and draw fine spiritual distinctions, and will continue to use ambiguous words in their common, conventional meaning without advertence or care for the misunderstanding that may arise.

This ambiguity is most obvious and most general in the use of the phrase "contemplative life". Originally signifying the higher reaches of the mental pursuits of a philosopher, it was transferred in the patristic period to the life of a monk or solitary devoted solely to prayer and other religious exercises. Later still, it was transferred again to the meditative study of Scripture that was the goal of the instruction given to the younger members of many religious houses. From this meaning came the normal use of the word in medieval and modern ecclesiastical language to denote the way of life of institutes and persons who are not engaged in pastoral, charitable, educational or scientific work of any kind, but whose occupation is primarily liturgical and private prayer, and whose study is primarily devotional. The life of the monastery presupposed by the Rule of St Benedict, and still more that of such an institute as the Charterhouse or the Carmelite order of nuns, is of this type, and with regard to such the expression "contemplative life" is a comprehensible and useful one, so long as it is understood in its everyday, conventional, nontechnical sense. When used thus in common parlance there is no immediate danger of confusing the contemplative life of the institute with the mystical life of its members, and those treating of the latter will either avoid the former term in this context or at least make a verbal distinction between the two.

It is less easy to adjust satisfactorily the slightly different use of the word by medieval and later theologians of the scholastic tradition. In their writings "contemplation" is often used of the reflection upon or penetration of revealed truth by the mind of the theologian or the student; in this they merely give a particular and scholastic character to the meditative reading of the monks of earlier days. The well-known adage that reading leads to meditation and meditation to contemplation, which is itself a misleading version of a more correct original,[1] reflects this meaning of the word, as does in a purely theological context the expression of Aquinas that the duty of a religious who is a theologian is himself to contemplate and then to pass on to others the issue of his contemplation.[2] The "contemplation" of these two pronouncements is not mystical contemplation in the full sense of those words, though each has in fact often been misapplied as if referring to mystical, infused knowledge. On the other hand (and this is evidence of the difficulty of vocabulary in this field), the contemplation here intended is not merely the term or result of a human, scientific investigation of a doctrine or a sacred subject. It is the luminous penetration of divine truth by a mind fully endowed with the supernatural intellectual virtues of a Christian, and able with their help to capture something of the spiritual meaning of the words of Christ and the writings of the apostles. These are gifts beyond price, and their influence upon the mind can be such as we see in the writings of St Thomas Aquinas and St Bonaventure among many others, who attain a spiritual depth and clarity which make their words at once perfectly comprehensible in matter and expression and yet convey to a mind in harmony with them the overtones of heavenly wisdom. But such knowledge is mystical only in a very broad sense of the term, for if the words in any particular case are based upon an experience of a higher nature, they fail to transmit or express it. Mystical contemplation is something far different from this.

Even in the field of prayer, its own proper field in the

[1] "Seek by reading and you will find in meditation; knock in prayer and the door will be opened to you in contemplation" (*Scala Claustralium* by Guigo II, prior of the Grande Chartreuse, in Migne, *Patrologia Latina*, 184, col. 476.

[2] *Summa Theologiae* IIa–IIae, qu. 188, art. 6, corp.

modern use of words, the term contemplation is equivocal. Leaving aside the use of the word for the final part of a set exercise of meditation, there is a long history of controversy, extending over more than three centuries, over the use of the adjectives "perfect", "infused" and "acquired" as applied to contemplation, and the permissibility of using, or restricting the use of, the single word contemplation in respect of each of these three expressions. We need not be detained by the discussion over "perfect" contemplation; it concerns the meaning of the term as used by several Spanish mystical writers, and in particular by St Teresa, and is not of general significance.

The other two expressions are of more practical interest. The first, "infused contemplation", needs no long treatment. It is, on the view adopted throughout this book, a tautology. Contemplation, in the context of personal prayer, is by definition freely infused knowledge and love. In the brief phrase of St John of the Cross, "contemplation is to receive".[3] If this is so, it must follow that "acquired contemplation" is a contradiction in terms. It is, indeed, an unfortunate expression which arose at a time and in a region when the ambiguities of the word contemplation had not been fully explored. In recent years spiritual writers have preferred to use the terms "active" and "infused recollection". But apart from purely verbal discussions, there is a real point of importance at issue, which must be considered briefly.

In the scheme of the degrees of prayer, which forms part of almost every recent discussion of mysticism or contemplation, the lowest step is composed of the prayer, called in the context the prayer of beginners, which is in fact the prayer of all Christians who are not in what may be called technically "the mystical way". It is the prayer in which meditation, reflection or reading, assisted imperceptibly by the grace that

---

[3] *Living Flame* (second redaction), stanza iii, par. 36 (*Complete Works of St John of the Cross*, ed. E. A. Peers, III, p. 162).

precedes and accompanies all good activities of the powers
of the soul, issues in "acts"; that is, conscious movements of
the mind and will in the direction of faith and love and
adoration. This is fully "active" prayer. But it must be remembered that while schematically the division between active and
infused love and knowledge is clear-cut, in ordinary life, as
opposed to theory and logic, growth is slow and gradual. In
nature, the difference between a seed and a plant is obvious
and essential, but there is a time of change in which both
the seed and the first shoots of the plant are present, the
former disappearing, the latter just visible. So in the matter
of prayer explicit words and thoughts, and even express "acts"
of faith and love, become more and more simple, until there
comes a time when prayer is to a greater or less degree one
of "loving attention" to God present in the mind as the object
of faith and hope and love. This is the degree known as the
"prayer of simplicity" or of "simple regard". There is nothing
overtly mystical about it, and those who practise it can, at
least normally, embark on it at will. Yet at the same time (and
this is of great significance, though it is often ignored), this
kind of prayer is not one that all devout persons can practise
or indeed understand. It is, in its fully developed form, the
prayer that accompanies a stage of spiritual growth. It is in
fact, though not perceptibly mystical or infused, more spiritual
and less mechanical than the prayer of expressed acts. There
will be occasion to return to this later, and for the moment it
is enough to have suggested that the spiritual nature of this
prayer and its imperceptible character tend to make it a
matter of controversy, and that there is reason, though not
perhaps adequate reason, for calling it "acquired contemplation". Yet in this use the word contemplation has no clear
significance, unless we suppose a confusion, which some
writers betray, between obscure, loving attention to the
presence of God and the moment of the mind's rest after a
process of meditation or reasoning. In fact, it would psycho-

logically be more correct to say, with St John of the Cross, that a succession in the past of express acts directed to God has produced a habit which enables the individual to be at will in the state to which these acts lead. It is certainly not infused contemplation, and has perhaps received more attention from spiritual writers than it deserves, for it is not a mystical prayer in the full sense of the word.

CHAPTER IV

THE MYSTICAL WAY AND SPIRITUAL GROWTH

To those who regard mysticism as merely a variety of psychological or religious experience the mystical way will have no necessary connection with ethical or spiritual excellence. Even Catholic theologians and spiritual writers can be found who maintain that mystical experiences, even those that are admitted to be genuinely spiritual and not merely autogenous or imaginary, are no more bound up with growth in holiness than are visions and locutions and other experiences which, however authentic and significant they may be, are to be ranked with the extraordinary graces and favours, the so-called *gratiae gratis datae* that are catalogued by St Paul, rather than with the sanctifying grace of the love of God. If, on the other hand, as has been held consistently in these pages, true mystical experiences are infusions of purifying and sanctifying grace, the question must be answered in another way. It is a question of real importance, for apart from those who dismiss mystical experiences as falling in a category apart from sanctifying grace and base their opinion upon reasons of a theological character, there are numerous writers who, without recourse to theological argument, show themselves unwilling to allow that mystical experience has any intimate connection with spiritual worth, and who are still more unwilling to allow that mystical perfection is the highest form of Christian excellence.

Some of the theological reasons for regarding the mystical way as an extension, a prolongation of the life of Christian virtue have already been given. The writers of the other class just mentioned base their conviction—or rather, support their opinion—on some assertions of the mystics themselves. St Teresa of Avila, in particular, is a storehouse of passages quoted in this sense. Of all the mystics, she is the most homely, the most human and in many ways the most informative. She is also the most diffuse, the most formless and the most inconsequent. She wrote at odd moments, without re-reading the previous pages, and often with long intervals between one chapter and another. She wrote rapidly and with the utmost personal candour, but with the needs and characters of her readers dictating her topics, and with all the humility of an untrained mind and of a woman in the Spain of the golden age of theology and of the Inquisition, conscious of her own mistakes and unfaithfulnesses in the past. The mother of a large and ever-growing family, containing more than its average quota of those with high spiritual gifts, but with its balance of nuns of ordinary attainments, of narrow minds and restless dispositions, she was concerned to impress upon her daughters the basic virtues of humility and obedience, and to prevent any misunderstanding of the unusual or lofty experiences of her own life. For these reasons, and many more, it is necessary to compare her judgements one with another, to consider their context and her motives in writing, and to remember that she wrote without the assistance of the training in exact theological thought of her ally St John of the Cross, and that, while he had read her works, she had not had the advantage of reading his.

To consider St Teresa's teaching at any length would demand long and critical exposition. Her basic outlook on the relationship of spiritual purity and the contemplative life, however, admits of no dispute. She presents it most clearly in *The Way of Perfection*, in which she wrote of prayer for her first small community of the Reform: "I will mention three things that must be done by those who intend to lead a life of prayer . . . the first of these is love for one another; the second, detachment from all created things; the other is true humility, which . . . includes the rest."[1]

In what follows, she returns more than once to the second necessary condition. It is the specific preparation for the evangelical life; it is the "active night" of St John of the Cross. She repeats, in her celebrated simile of the game of chess:

> This King will not let Himself be taken, except by one who is entirely given up to Him. . . . If we do not yield ourselves to Him as entirely as He gives Himself to us, He does what suffices by leaving us to mental prayer [as contrasted with contemplation] and visiting us now and then.[2]

Later she returns to the subject in words of great energy:

> The chief point is that we should resolutely give Him our heart for His own, and should empty it of everything else. . . . This is the condition He makes, and He is right in doing so: do not let us refuse it Him. . . . As Christ does not force our wills, He only takes what we give Him, but He does not give Himself entirely until He sees that we yield ourselves entirely to Him. This is an undoubted truth, which I insist upon so often because of its great importance.[3]

Elsewhere she writes, in words which remind us of the exhortation of Walter Hilton to the pilgrim to Jerusalem:

> Pay no heed, then, to anyone who tries to frighten you or depicts to you the perils of the way. What a strange idea that one could ever expect to travel on a road infested by thieves, for the purpose of gaining some great treasure, without running

---

[1] *Way of Perfection* IV (*The Complete Works of St Teresa of Jesus*, translated and edited by E. Allison Peers, Volume II, 16).

[2] *Way of Perfection XVI* (Peers II, 66).

[3] Ibid., XXVIII (Peers II, 118).

into danger! Worldly people like to take life peaceably; but they will deny themselves sleep for nights on end in order to gain a farthing's profit, and they will leave you no peace either of body or of soul.[4]

St John of the Cross has the same message, put in words of still greater force:

> Oh, that one might show us how to understand, practise and experience what this counsel is which our Saviour here [Mark 8. 34–5] gives us concerning the denial of ourselves, so that spiritual persons might see in how different a way they should conduct themselves upon this road from that which many of them think proper. For they believe that any kind of retirement and reformation of life suffices; and others are content with practising the virtues and continuing in prayer and pursuing mortification; but they attain not to detachment and poverty or denial or spiritual purity, which the Lord here commends to us.[5]

Enough has surely been seen of these two pillars of the contemplative life in the modern world to make it quite clear that, for them, the mystic is one who has served a severe apprenticeship and reached a high degree of moral and spiritual purity.

The question we have been considering is closely bound up with another, that of the relative excellence of the "active" and "contemplative" lives. To give this distinction any meaning we may substitute for active and contemplative the less ambiguous terms of mystical and non-mystical. Setting aside the endless discussions as to whether any really devout life is "non-mystical", we are here considering a serious problem reduced to its essentials. Does the authentic mystic attain a higher level of supernatural virtue than that reached by active, ascetic perseverance? The answer, based both on spiritual

[4] Ibid., XXI (Peers II, 90).
[5] *Ascent of Mount Carmel* II, 7 (*The Complete Works of St John of the Cross*, translated and edited by E. Allison Peers, Volume I, 84).

reasons and the declarations of the mystics themselves, must emphatically be Yes, with the reservation that we are speaking of the fully-grown mystic at the term of his life. If Christian perfection is to be found in the union of the human will with that of God (the will of the Father and of the Son) a far stronger, closer and more permanent union is achieved when God moves and holds the intellect and will by his direct control in the soul's centre than when an individual acts, with grace indeed inspiring, aiding and moving, but by means of the normal human deliberate conjunction of reason and will. Put in another way, this is to say that the soul and its powers cannot have the purity and the strength to receive the supreme bestowal of union unless they have been refined and strengthened by the tests and tonic medicine of physical and mental suffering or the mystical purifications of darkness and trial.

Nevertheless, when we judge in the concrete, not in the abstract, other considerations must play their part. Indeed, we may think that it does not befit a human being to pronounce upon his equals or to use such phrases as absolute or comparative perfection in virtue when speaking of destinies which are governed by God's inscrutable providence and his free, all-loving distribution of his gifts. Clearly, also, a mystical life in its early stages will not show the mature strength of a long life of apostolic virtue. And who shall say, in the concrete case of a saintly life, whether the mystical element is present or not? Perhaps the only real point of importance is to oppose firmly any suggestion that an entirely "active", non-mystical life of virtue may surpass in excellence the fullest mystical union.

Closely allied, and perhaps more practical than this question is the more common and general one: are there then two distinct ways of perfection for Christians, the "active" and the "contemplative"? Tradition at first sight, and perhaps also on a longer view, answers Yes, and is likewise unquestioned in asserting the superiority of the contemplative life, which from the days of St Augustine to the present has been seen as that commended by our Lord as the better part, when represented by Mary, the sister of Lazarus. It is true that tradition has been confused by the ambiguity of the word "contemplative", which for a millennium was equated with the monastic life, at that time universally recognized as a higher life, and a higher state, than that of life "in the world". But even when this ambiguity disappeared in the later Middle Ages the traditional teaching preferred the contemplative, mystical life as such to the active life of works. Thus the author of *The Cloud of Unknowing* could write:

> Since all the men of this life may be divided into three: in sinners, in actives and in contemplatives, therefore generally ... this word of our Lord may be said unto all: "Without me"—either only suffering [i.e. permitting] and not consenting, as in sinners; or both suffering and consenting, as in actives; or (that more than all this is) principally stirring and working, as in contemplatives—"ye may do nothing".[6]

And he insists:

> Of one thing I warn thee ... and especially in this place where I make a difference between them that be called to salvation and them that be called to perfection: that of whichever part thou feelest thy calling to be, look that thou neither judge nor discuss in the deeds of God nor of man further than only thyself.... If thou be called [to perfection] give praising unto God and pray that thou fail not. And if thou be not yet called, pray meekly to God that he call thee when his will is.... Have peace with the part, whichever thou have. Thou needest not to complain, for they be both precious. The first is good and needeth always to be had; the second is better, get it whoso get it may; or (as I shall trulier say) whoso by grace is gotten and called thereto by our Lord.[7]

It will have been noticed that this master tacitly equates the contemplative life with the life of the perfect fulfilment

[6] *The Epistle of Privy Counsel*, ed. J. McCann, p. 226.
[7] Ibid. pp. 222–6.

of the divine commandments, and by the contemplative life he names what we have called the mystical life. The modern world, and even the modern religious world, has not been willing to accept this position without protest. From the time of the Counter-Reformation to the present day spiritual writers have been divided into those who subordinate their ascetical teaching to the later demands of the mystical life, and those whose approach is by way of activity and authority. During these centuries first one and then the other attitude has prevailed in this region or that and has formed the climate of the times. Only in the past fifty years has there been a semblance of agreement on a compromise—a semblance only, for the antagonism, if latent, still exists. It is worth while to look for a moment at this division and its causes.

The conviction, amounting to a tradition, that the mystical life was the goal and crown of the active life, that it was the life of the perfect as opposed to that of the proficient, and that in consequence it was the "normal" way of Christian sanctity, and as such within the purview of all devout Christians as an end to be striven for, desired and prayed for, was unquestionably the common opinion of spiritual writers from the earliest days of monasticism till the century before the Reformation. Undoubtedly it derived much of its authority from the adoption by all theologians, mystical as well as dogmatic, of the Neoplatonic categories of spiritual growth according to which contemplation, issuing ultimately in ecstasy, was set up as the goal and crown of the spiritual life. Translated into purely religious and Christian terms, this programme divided all believers into three classes: that of sinful, nominal Christians; that of sincere believers actively practising the virtues; and that of contemplatives, embryo and mature. Though repeated for centuries, these categories were bookish, and the veneration of all the faithful was extended to many who were recognized as saints without having, so far as could be seen, passed through the contemplative life. Saints such as St Louis of France, St Margaret of Scotland and martyrs, real or supposed, were more numerous than the monastic saints in some periods and regions. But as most of the sainted bishops had spent their early life in the monastery, and as even lay devotion in the eleventh and twelfth centuries was cast in the monastic mould, there was no serious break in tradition, and the scholastics, most of them friars, canonized it, though by creating a third category, the mixed life, they were able to include their own institutes, with the proviso (itself deriving ultimately from Plotinus) that action was in one way a preparation for, and in another way the overflowing of, contemplation. Till the fourteenth century, therefore, the old tradition persisted. It is mirrored in Walter Hilton's *Ladder of Perfection* where, as in *The Cloud of Unknowing*, the dichotomy into "actives" and "contemplatives", the superiority of the latter, and the universal invitation to contemplation are assumed as needing neither explanation nor defence. Hilton writes:

> Men may be classed in various categories according to the various states of the soul. Some are not reformed to the likeness of God, and some are reformed only in faith, and some are reformed in faith and feeling.... Reform in faith is the lowest state of elect souls, below which they cannot well be, and reform in feeling is the highest state that a soul can come to in this life. But a soul cannot suddenly spring from the lowest to the highest.... No man suddenly receives the highest graces, but he may attain them through long exercises.[8]

The fifteenth and sixteenth centuries brought about a great change of sentiment and doctrine, here as elsewhere. The revolution in philosophy and theology, associated with the name of Ockham and later known as Nominalism, destroyed over a large area the traditional doctrine of grace as a direct

[8] *The Scale of Perfection*, ed. G. Sitwell, Book II, chapters 13 and 17, pp. 174, 183.

contact between God and man, and as establishing a new principle of life with new potencies and powers of growth, and the possibility of a new knowledge and love of God. There was a time-lag of a century or more before the negative influence of the new way of thought reached the spiritual writers, but it can be felt rather than seen in the *Imitation of Christ*, which preserves the traditional phrases while avoiding a theological presentation of the contemplative life. Soon the decadence of the monastic life in many regions, the attacks of Wyclif and others, and the return to a supposedly purer early Christian simplicity as pictured in different ways by Colet and Erasmus, all combined to break the prestige of the monks. Finally the attack of the Reformers on the ideals of a vowed life following the evangelical counsels, and the crying need, in both the Old World and the New, for apostles and preachers, combined to create a new "image" of Christian perfection and sanctity. This was realized in the lives of a series of saintly men, Cajetan, Ignatius, Francis Xavier and the rest, living and preaching lives of mental and physical activity, in which external heroism and enterprise, and visible works of charity to mind and body, took the place of the "fugitive and cloistered virtue" alike in Catholic and in Protestant circles. The theological, theoretical justification for the new spirituality was developed most comprehensively by the Jesuits, who for almost two centuries commanded a large proportion of the zeal and learning of Catholic Europe.

Yet in the same epoch of Reform a revival had taken place, at first chiefly in Spain, the spiritual home of the Jesuits, of traditional theology and of monastic spirituality, and just as the Jesuit cause had been immensely strengthened by their galaxy of saints in the first decades of their existence, so the traditional mystical life received powerful external advocacy in the persons of the two Carmelite saints, Teresa and John of the Cross, with their associates and disciples. Their Order and their writings spread rapidly and a number of religious in other institutes, and saintly priests and bishops adopted their teaching, especially in France and the Netherlands.

Henceforth we can see a double polarity in Catholic teaching on the spiritual life, represented by what may roughly, if imprecisely, be called the mystical and the ascetic schools of spirituality. In this confrontation neither party could claim a monopoloy in holiness of life or intangible purity of doctrine, and there were many instances of divided allegiance. While the party of the mystical tradition suffered from the extravagances of the Illuminists and Quietists, and while many of their number adopted the devotional practices introduced by the Society of Jesus, their rivals were accused of novel opinions on grace and conduct by both the theologians and moralists, even before Jansenism confused all issues, while some of their eminent masters, such as Fathers Lallemant and Surin, adopted much of the teaching of the Spanish Carmelites. St Francis de Sales showed in his earlier work a strong "ascetical" colour which changed in his later writings, through his association with the nuns of the Visitation, to a more "mystical" tone. Later, Fathers de Caussade and Grou took a middle way which, if anything, turned in a "mystical" direction.

If the eighteenth century saw a decline in both schools of spirituality, the nineteenth was on the whole turned towards the ascetic, "active" outlook, and the many new Orders, particularly those of women, adopted in varying measure the Ignatian constitutional and spiritual framework. The present century in its first half saw a notable revival of the contemplative Orders and of traditional mystical doctrine, while in recent decades there has been something of a *détente* in which all parties have made efforts to reach something like a compromise.

More will be said of this later. For the moment it is enough to remark that those who follow the traditional Jesuit teaching on the nature of grace will always find it difficult to admit as the touchstone of mystical experience the capacity of a soul to be moved habitually by the inevitably efficacious, but freely received, intrinsic "operant" grace, while the Dominicans are equally unwilling to accept the possibility of two ways or modes of Christian perfection, the "active" and the "mystical", whether they are regarded as equally meritorious, or whether the "mystical" way is regarded as something abnormal and occasional, if not wholly "extraordinary". Each opinion has its strength. The Dominican teaching is theologically the more convincing, though if pressed with rigidity it decreases in acceptability, as Aristotelian logic so often does, the further its conclusions are taken from the original principle. The Jesuit view, on the other hand, is in some ways more respectful of observed facts and experience and, if the opposing opinion is at all exaggerated, of common Christian sentiment. The theoretical dilemma, if indeed one exists, is presented by the mystics themselves. They insist with one voice upon the absolute and uncovenanted freedom of God to give or refuse the gift of contemplation without reference to the meritorious quality of precedent virtue. At the same time they insist upon the essential connection between true mystical experience and moral and spiritual purity. Thirdly, they are unanimous in asserting both the compulsive force and the free reception of the divine infusion of knowledge and love.

These three claims will be discussed and illustrated in the following chapter. Meanwhile, we may conclude this brief review by a judgement as follows. First, that in the long spiritual tradition of the Church the mystical way has been regarded as the end and crown of the life of grace by all writers previous to the Reformation, and by many since. Secondly, that theologians in unanimity until the fifteenth century, and in a majority since that time, have seen in the mystical life a prolongation, normal, if in fact uncommon, of the life of grace seen in the infused virtues and the Gifts of the Holy Ghost. Thirdly, that the mystical way differs in degree and in kind from the common life of Christian practice, and that the raising of a soul from one to the other is an uncovenanted gift of God.

CHAPTER V

ARE THERE TWO WAYS TO THE PERFECT CHRISTIAN LIFE?

In these pages the mystical life has been presented as a full expansion of the Christian life of grace, that is, of the infused, supernatural virtues of faith, hope and charity (the love of God), and of the powerful indwelling of the Holy Spirit, expressed by the traditional theology of the Gifts. Its goal is the goal of all serious Christian endeavour, that is, the love of God without measure, the perfect fulfilment of the commands of Christ, and of the spirit, at least, of his counsels, and the union of will with him. While we believe that any soul in a state of grace, that is, one who has faith in God and a firm intention of fulfilling his will in all important matters, will be saved by the merits of Christ, it would be absurd to hold that such a limited attitude towards God and Christ's Gospel should be the ideal and goal of all those who have heard Christ's call and have meditated upon his life and Passion. There is a real call, a real obligation on all Christians to love God with all the powers and faculties of their being.

If anything is clear from the writings of the mystics, whether those who speak only of their own experience or of those who write to instruct others, it is that their principal, indeed their sole, aim is to escape from self-love and to give themselves wholly to Christ, the Son of God. They do not ask or desire—indeed, they deprecate all such asking or desiring—any extraordinary powers, any unusual divine instructions, any sight or vision of Christ. They ask only God's help to identify themselves with Christ in his love of the Father and of all men. They follow the path that all must follow if they would see God, but they follow it to the summit of the mountain.

But while we may agree that the mystical way is a clear if eminent way of Christian perfection, and however unusual is not theologically speaking extraordinary, there still remains the further question—is it the only way of Christian perfection? Granted that a Christian sincerely desires with God's help to love him with all his powers and to dedicate and sacrifice to God all that fallen human nature desires to keep "as its own", is the mystical way the only way in which this can be realized?

From what we have seen, the mystics themselves appear at first sight to say "Yes". The whole burden of the writings of Tauler, of Hilton, of St John of the Cross seems to equate the mystical life with the perfect Christian life, with the fullest possible development here below of the eternal life that begins with baptism and ends in the Beatific Vision. And a great school of theologians, basing itself directly upon St Thomas and the unbroken series of his commentators and indirectly (but validly) upon patristic and medieval tradition, has given its support to the mystics in this.

Against this teaching two main lines of argument have developed. The first is not so much an argument as a revolt of commonsense. Are we to believe that Christian perfection in its fullest development is to be found only in a minute group, of whom not one in ten thousand Christians has any knowledge, whose lives (as it appears) are passed in a spiritual atmosphere of extreme rarity, often accompanied by unusual trials and moments of vision? And are all Christians commanded or invited to direct their desires and energies in this direction? Such considerations have considerable force at first appearance, but in fact they could be used to demolish any lofty conception of Christian endeavour. Were not the great saints of the Church also men and women? Are we not to take their faith and love of God as our ideal and example? Are they a numerous band? Are all their actions sensible and their lives peaceful and sunny? Are we prepared to face their renunciations? Were not many of them mystics? And as for the extraordinary, unfamiliar and even seemingly distasteful aspects of the mystical life, were not similar characteristics a stumbling-block to the contemporaries of the apostles—a crucified God, a Virgin Mother, the call to poverty and humility, the elements of the miraculous, the charismatic and the apocalyptic? It is only familiarity and childhood indoctrination that allow us to accept without a tremor these elements of our faith and of the Christian life.

A more telling argument is the complete accord of mystics and theologians that the passage from the common Christian exercise of faith and love, and from the experience and effort of grace-aided virtuous action, and from what Hilton calls reformation in faith, to the reception of infused love and knowledge, the reformation in feeling—to say nothing of the higher, rarer stages of the mystical life—that this change is purely and absolutely God's work, and cannot be achieved, or even in the strict sense of the word merited by man. We may hear them insist upon this:

> It is the work of only God, wrought in whatever soul he liketh, without any merit of the same soul. For without it no saint nor angel can think to desire it ... and yet he giveth not this grace, nor worketh this work, in a soul that is unable thereto. And yet there is no soul without this grace, which is

able to have [i.e. capable of itself to have] this grace; none, whether it be a sinner's soul or an innocent soul.[1]

God is free and gives Himself to whom He wills and when He wills, not for any particular work [i.e. meritorious work] or at any particular time. Though a soul does all in its power for a lifetime, it will never have perfect [i.e., infused, mystical] love of Jesus till He freely gives it.[2]

This prayer is something supernatural to which no effort of our own can raise us ... it is supernatural and utterly beyond our control ... which no skill or effort of ours, however much we labour, can attain to.[3]

And it was a happy chance [the phrase is taken from the poem "In a dark night"] that God should lead the soul into this night [sc. the passive night of sense] for of itself the soul would not have succeeded in entering therein.[4]

God grants these favours to whom He wills and for what reason He wills. For it may come to pass that a person will have performed many good works, yet that He will not give these touches of His favour; and another will have done far fewer good works, yet He will give him them to a most sublime degree.[5]

Yet at the same time all admit and indeed proclaim that the gift is given most frequently to those who have prepared themselves to receive it:

Surely God will not give such a grace except to a man who, for his part, does all that is in his power, and would do still more, if he knew how.[6]

But no casual preparation will suffice:

Why is it that so few ever attain to this state [of the perfection of union with God]? It must be known that it is not

[1] *The Cloud of Unknowing*, ed. J. McCann, XXXIV, 83–4.

[2] *Scale* II, XXXIV, 189–90.

[3] St Teresa, *Spiritual Relation V* (Peers I, 216). The quotation is from the translation by David Lewis (ed. B. Zimmerman) where it figures as Relation VIII.

[4] *Ascent* I, i (Peers I, 19).

[5] Ibid., II, xxxii (Peers I, 208).

[6] *Scale* II, xx, 190·

because God is pleased that there should be few raised to this high spiritual state, for it would rather please Him that all souls should be perfect ... but there are many who desire to make progress and constantly entreat God to bring them to this state of perfection ... and when it pleases God to bring them through the first trials and mortifications as is necessary, they are unwilling to pass through them, and flee away ...[7]

And yet these masters do not cease to invite their readers to press forward to the goal of mystical union. Doubtless we must remember that all those whom we are quoting have made it clear that they are writing for individuals or groups who have chosen, and who are practising in good heart, a life of a strictly disciplined character. But there is no mistaking the purpose behind Hilton's celebrated parable of the pilgrim to Jerusalem, or of St Teresa's eloquent, impetuous chapter (xxi) in *The Way of Perfection*, or of St John's outburst in *The Living Flame*:

Oh souls that seek to walk in security and comfort in spiritual things! If ye did but know how necessary it is to suffer and to endure in order to reach this security and consolation, ye would in no way seek consolation either from God or from creatures, but would rather bear the cross ... and would count this a great happiness ... and bearing a few outward things with patience and faithfulness, ye would become worthy for God to set His eyes upon you, to purge and cleanse you more inwardly by means of more interior spiritual trials [*sc.* the night of the spirit] and to give you more interior blessings. For they to whom God is to grant so notable a favour as to try them more interiorly ... must have rendered Him many services, and have had much patience and constancy for His sake.[8]

[7] *The Living Flame of Love* (2nd redaction), Stanza II, par. 27 (Peers III, 138).
[8] Ibid., par. 28 (Peers III, 139).

And for this reason, the number of contemplatives is small, and the higher the degree of union, the smaller the number.

> The night of sense is common, and the lot of many [he is speaking of Carmelite nuns and friars]...the night of the spirit is the portion of the very few.[9]

And again:

> Not all, speaking generally, pass into it [*sc.* the night of the spirit] but only the smallest number.[10]

And, more precisely and more solemnly:

> Not all those who walk of set purpose in the way of the spirit are brought by God to contemplation...nor even the half of them—why, He best knows.[11]

The last three words have often been discussed. Do they refer immediately or only remotely to the inscrutable designs of God's providence and predestination? Or does St John himself give the answer on another page?

> And thus they give God no opportunity by submitting to the smallest trials. To these may be made the reply, "If thou hast run with the footmen, and they have wearied thee, how canst thou contend with horses? And if in the land of peace they wearied thee, then how wilt thou do in the swelling of Jordan?"[12]

For many are called, but few are chosen.

In the last analysis we are brought into the mystery of man's freewill and the inscrutable providence of God. In the universe of being as it exists for the eye to see and for the mind to consider, there is an intricate hierarchy from simplicity to complexity, from the electron to man, and within each species there is a variety of excellence. Star differeth from star in glory; rose from rose in beauty; yet each has its place in the divine ordination. So with men; the native

[9] *The Dark Night of the Soul*, I, viii (Peers I, 349).
[10] Ibid., I, xiv (Peers I, 371–2).
[11] Ibid. I, ix (Peers I, 356).
[12] *Living Flame* (2nd redaction), II, 27 (Peers III, 128–9).

of New Guinea is as truly a human being as Plato or Augustine, yet the immediate existential capacity for knowledge and for influence over others is so varied in different individuals. This we admit, however grudgingly, even in the egalitarian climate of our day. So it is with men, regarded as the twice-born children of God. All indeed are loved by him as individuals, and as if no other individual existed, but there is no flat rate of love. The love of God for the individual soul, and the God-given love of the soul for God, differ with infinite variety within the human race. Here indeed we touch a mystery that does not exist in roses, the conflict in our mind between the free-will of the individual and the predestined certainty of grace and glory that God has from all eternity reserved for his chosen ones, but in the tangible realm of experience the differences of life-span, environment, character and also of grace remain. We know that we have grace sufficient (in the everyday sense of the word) to keep us in God's love to the end; we know that we are commanded to love God to the full extent of our capacity; we know also (and God himself has said it) that our capacities and spiritual gifts are unequal, as is also the measure of the light of glory in store for the elect. We know too, that God has willed this variety, this inequality, from all eternity, though we know not why he has willed it. It will exist among the blessed, it has existed among saints and perfect souls during this life. In the last resort variety is not inequality, for all is as God has predestined. Many, no doubt, were called to the mystical way and have failed to hear and answer the call. Others, his best beloved, have been flooded with grace from infancy and have responded without failing. Much is given to them, because they have loved much, and they have loved much because they have received much love. As it hath pleased the Lord, so hath he done.

CHAPTER VI

VISIONS AND ECSTASIES

Many of those who, both in the past and in the present, have read the lives and writings of the saints and mystics, and especially those who know of Catholic piety only from outside and superficially, regard visions, ecstasies, raptures, locutions and the like, either for better or for worse, as the inevitable accompaniment and signature of sanctity and of the mystical life. Some regard such things with admiration, others with dislike. The same difference of opinion has existed in the past even among Catholic writers. Some have made much of these and other supposed manifestations of divine favour, or have at least expatiated on the rules for judging between true and false visions. Others, in a steady stream from the earliest times, have insisted that visions and locutions are in themselves neither a part of the mystical life nor an evidence of sanctity. This latter opinion, which can now be called the common teaching of mystical theologians and spiritual writers, may be accepted in theory and practice, but the problem remains: if these manifestations or experiences are in fact authentic, what is their purpose and value?

We may begin by noting that as Christians and believers in the omnipotence and universal providence of God we must maintain the possibility of the Creator communicating with his creatures in any way he may choose. We are not here questioning or discussing communications of any sort conveyed by God to man in the course of divine revelation. Nor would we deny that Christ, who truly associated with his disciples after his resurrection, and spoke of the kingdom of God within them, could do so at other times, as it is possible that he did in the case of St Paul, though it is the common and traditional opinion of theologians that he has never in fact since the ascension been seen on earth in human form. Nor, if we admit the existence in God's creation of pure spirits good and evil would we deny the possibility that they could be employed by God to convey a message in a manner that could be received by a human being. Nor would we exclude the possibility that the human spirit, and especially the human spirit refined by purifying grace, could be aware, on the spiritual level, of contact with a good or evil spiritual being. At the same time we know, both from the teaching of Christ and from Scripture and tradition, that the normal and indeed the only way to be expected of God's action is by the internal and imperceptible action of the Holy Spirit. What, then, is to be said of the visions of saints and mystics? Why should they not be regarded as a normal accompaniment, or indeed one of the graces, of the mystical way?

Firstly, no doubt, because of the common human experiences of hallucination and self-deception, not to speak of fraud. Everyone has read of instances of all these, and some will have had first-hand experience. Morbid psychologists and psychiatrists are here well within their lawful territory. However difficult a perfectly normal mind may find it to conceive of a self-induced and yet *bona fide* picture in the imagination which is accepted as an objective, external appearance, yet such hallucinations (to give them a non-technical name) are relatively frequent phenomena. Secondly, within the context of a secluded religious life, persons liable to such mental processes multiply them unendingly and, the more complete their self-deception and apparent *bona fides*, the more confusion do they cause to themselves and others.

But, we may be told, *abusus non tollit usum*, the counterfeit should not prejudice the sincere. What of visions and words which are in fact "authentic", that is, which are seen or heard by persons of known integrity and virtue, or which carry in themselves a guarantee by reason of their theological or spiritual truth and sublimity, and their good effect upon the subject concerned, as, for example, the instructions which St Catherine of Siena accepted as spoken by Christ, or the words heard by Dame Julian of Norwich? To answer this we must speak for a moment theologically. What is strictly supernatural, that is, what is in any way part of the life of God either in himself or as imparted in sanctifying grace to the soul, cannot in any way fall under the cognizance of the human senses or understanding. Consequently, that which in any way falls under such cognizance is not immediately and directly a divine communication. The axiom that whatever is given can only be received according to the capacity of the recipient is valid here. God can touch directly the obediential receptivity of the soul in sanctifying grace, but when the communication is transmitted to the mind or imagination these powers may translate the message according to their own powers of reception as a picture or a sequence of words. Thus a whole reel of visions, such as those of Catherine Emmerich, if not wholly autogenous or morbid, is at best a superficial reflection of an impression which the soul itself was incapable of receiving fully, and a sequence of words is the reaction of the understanding to a stimulus which may be so spiritual as to be scarcely perceived by the will.

Words, thoughts and imaginations are the end-product of a deeper, inarticulate process even in the affairs of daily life, and God, in whose hand are the hearts of kings, to turn like water whither he wills, desires always to give his gifts and himself to the deepest centre of the soul. It is only when the receptive powers are ill-attuned that his message rises upwards to the level of sense-perception and becomes inevitably confused and incomplete to a greater or less degree. So far from

being regarded as marvellous and supernatural, visions and
locutions of a definite, communicable kind are the weak outward signs, or the only and inadequate appearance, of what
could in itself have been a deeper enrichment of the soul. It is
for this reason, ultimately, that "visions" are to be reckoned
of no significance, not because a soul rejects any, even the
least, sign of God's presence, but because it turns immediately
to the invisible being always present in the soul and seen there
with the eyes of faith.

Ecstasies, raptures and the like have in themselves no
spiritual value. Leaving aside for the moment what may be
called philosophical ecstasy, the absorption of the mind in
the delight of some truth or intuition, we are considering the
alienation of the mind, often accompanied by symptoms of
trance or lifelessness, which are recorded or have in recent
times been observed in mystics real or supposed. In themselves, they resemble very closely some of the phenomena of
morbid psychology, and may often in fact be no different
from these. Experience and observation, however, show that
what may justly be called an influence of a supernatural kind,
an awareness of the nearness of God, may have a reflex effect
on a spiritually immature person. The presence of divine
power, like a sudden access of great pain or great joy, can
overwhelm the faculties. In the experience of the mystics
themselves, however, and in the instructions of mystical theologians, there is agreement that such phenomena are a sign of
weakness and immaturity and vanish when the soul advances
to maturity. The same may be said of any of the other
psycho-somatic phenomena that bulk so large in older treatises
on the mystical life and in the researches of psychologists. In
the soul strengthened by God the purely supernatural can
enter without disturbance, and without itself losing its purity.

It is an equally great error to regard as marvellous and
supernatural what is in fact a symptom of physical or psychological weakness, and to attach importance to nothing but

material things and label all visions as morbid, or hallucination. The visible signs of themselves tell nothing of their cause, and a low conception of the supernatural, and a materialistic denial of its existence, are equally far from a true presentation of the fact behind the appearances. The practical problem remains of distinguishing between fraudulent, self-deceiving, morbid and entirely sincere personalities. It is a difficult problem, but no more difficult than any judgement of character based only on appearances. In the last analysis, judgement must follow results. Grapes cannot be plucked from thistles; by their fruits we may know them.

Nevertheless, it must always be remembered that the psyche, the delicate organization at the roots of all human faculties, is as subject to weakness and disease as is the body, and that the gifts of God are distributed according to his will and his unsearchable design. The soul destined for great things may be in origin psychologically infirm. It may even be possible, though it cannot be asserted, that the delicacy of the natural organism needed for the reception of spiritual energy is such that it has weaknesses that can be repaired only by spiritual force. There would seem to be some evidence that genius, and in particular supreme musical genius, is often found in personalities so delicately poised that the slightest jar throws them off balance. "Genius is sure to madness near allied." However this may be, it is certain that some of the greatest mystical saints have shown in early life, and sometimes for many years, clear symptoms of nervous instability. Here the criterion is once more a moral one, but it is essential to allow for the strengthening of mind and character under the influence of divine grace. St Teresa of Avila unquestionably showed signs in her early life of psychological unbalance and instability, but the mature woman was as unquestionably strong, sane and self-controlled. Mystics, as is clear both from their own statements and from theological principles, have to pass through trials and tensions of which others have no conception. It is not surprising that strains and ruptures should occur, nor that the organism when fortified and inured to suffering should show a superhuman strength. It is not to be expected that those who do not accept the existence of a personal, loving Creator and Father will accept the healing power of grace, still less the mystics' teaching of the intellectual and moral purification achieved by the dark and painful experience of the excess of divine light and love in the imperfect faculties of the soul, but it is right to assert what is the teaching alike of mystics and theologians in this matter.

Having said so much, it is well also to remember that all discussion of mystical theology is, for those outside the number of the mystics, in many ways a matter of fumbling in the dark, and that we must always be ready to learn from the mystics themselves. Nor are we, or they, competent to decide what God does or should do in matters where he gives freely what he wills to whom he wills. A physician may know his anatomy, his bacteriology, his biochemistry, and his facts of disease and its symptoms, but in the final decision upon an individual case he must observe what is presented to his judgement in concrete form and judge by observation and direct information. So must we allow the words and the actions of the mystics to be put in evidence before we roundly pronounce, even upon such a matter as visions. It is easy for those far outside the pale of contemplative prayer to judge this and that to be useless and unworthy of a saint. The dealings of God with a soul are, in sober truth, out of our ken and none of our business. We have light only to see our own infirmity. "Visions" and such may well stand to the progressing soul as natural aids to devotion stand to the workaday Christian.

If he is lost in church without the aesthetic aids of architecture, music and emotional excitement his faith is clearly weak, and if he hopes to grow he must prepare himself to pray in surroundings which neither soothe nor please. What is born of the flesh is flesh, and no natural beauty has any power of itself to sanctify. On the other hand, all created beauty can help to set the soul on its course to God and it is puritanism and Jansenism that would deprive all Christians of all natural and physical amenities in the service of God. It is for the individual in all humility and silence to shut out the lower beauty that he may see the higher. So for many on the way to God help may be needful for the moment that others, at other times, would do well to renounce or to transcend. The multiple visions and locutions of St Teresa, even if some were in part the work of her own faculties unable as yet to accept stronger food, may have been an allowable, even a necessary, means of leading her towards a higher goal. It is not for others who have not even the beginnings of her love of Christ to condemn her. The most that can be said—and in fact she says it herself—is that the only true mysticism is that in which God alone fills the powers of the soul, and as God can be neither seen, heard, felt nor conceived as he is, the soul, if it is striving to attain to God alone, must pass by and transcend everything that is distinctly seen or felt, and remain in faith and love of the unseen. No mystical writer, not even St John of the Cross, has shown such a clear understanding of this matter as the Englishman Walter Hilton. He has been asserting very strongly that no soul that is not thoroughly purified can receive the infused knowledge and love of contemplation, and he feels it necessary to forestall an objection that may well have been made by those familiar with the writings of Richard Rolle and his school:

> But you may say, how can this be so? For there are many souls still at the beginning of their conversion who receive great spiritual favours. Some have ... spiritual light in their understanding; some again feel a consoling heat and great sweetness, and yet these souls never really enter this peaceful darkness [which Hilton has pronounced to be a necessary concomitant of contemplation] ... they never arrive at this ardent desire

and continual thought of God. You ask whether these souls are reformed in feeling [i.e. contemplatives, in Hilton's terminology] or not? It seems that they are, inasmuch as they have these exceptional spiritual experiences which other men, who are reformed only in faith [i.e., are not contemplatives], do not have. . . .

To this I say that it seems to me that these spiritual experiences . . . are not the experiences which will come to a soul by the grace of contemplation. I do not deny that they are genuine and the result of God's grace. But the souls which experience them are not yet reformed in feeling, and have not yet come to perfection nor to the burning spiritual love of Jesus that they may come to. And yet it often seems otherwise; that such souls feel more of the love of God than those who have attained perfection, inasmuch as their experience manifests itself much more exteriorly, in tears, . . . locutions and other bodily phenomena. So much so, that they seem to an onlooker to be continually in an ecstasy of love. And though I do not think that is so, I am aware that these experiences, the fervour of devotion and compunction that they feel, are gifts of God's grace granted to chosen souls to draw them from the love of the world. . . .

And yet the fervour which shows itself so strongly in exterior signs is not the result only of the greatness of their love; it is on account of the weakness of their souls, which are not able to bear the lightest touch of God. They are still, as it were, . . . entangled in the flesh, and not yet freed from it by the mortification of the spirit. And therefore the least touch of love or the smallest spark of spiritual light . . . is so great and consoling . . . that the soul is overwhelmed by it . . . [and] has not the strength to bear it, but breaks out in tears and other manifestations. Just as, when new wine . . . is put into an old barrel, the barrel swells and almost bursts . . . but when the wine has purified itself and cleared it does not work any more. . . . And so I say that these souls that feel such great bodily fervour, though they have great grace, are not yet reformed in feeling. . . The truth is, I think, that consolation and the fervour that a soul feels when it is in the state of a beginner . . .

are, as it were, spiritual food sent from heaven to strengthen it on the way.... And the same may be said of other sorts of phenomena that are physical in their nature, such as hearing sweet song, and the feeling of comfortable heat, or perceiving certain lights.... These are not spiritual experiences, for spiritual experiences occur in the powers of the soul, principally in the intellect and the will, and little in the imagination. But these experiences are in the imagination and therefore they are not spiritual. At their best they are only outward signs of the inner grace that is experienced in the powers of the soul.... It is not good for imperfect souls that have the sensible feelings, and have not yet received the interior grace, to rely too much on such feelings, but let them make use of them in so far as they help to fix the thought more steadily on God and to have greater love. For some of these experiences may be genuine and some false.[1]

I have quoted Hilton at some length as one of the earliest writers to meet the problem of visions and the like with a clear and theological explanation, maintaining on the one hand their purpose and validity, and on the other their derivative character even when "genuine", as the only form in which the purely spiritual grace can be received by a soul as yet tied to its exterior senses.

Hitherto, following an arrangement of the matter that has become common form, we have divided our subject into a twofold, sharp distinction of natural and supernatural, mystical and non-mystical. Without some such division and without a fairly sharp definition of terms, one cannot hope to reach any understanding on what is a difficult topic. We must not, however, forget two cardinal points. The first, and lesser, is that we are treating of human experience, that is to say, of the experience of individual human beings, none of whom exactly resembles his neighbour in situation, qualities, and eternal destiny. Any kind of classification of behaviour and experience must therefore necessarily be a step removed from

[1] *Scale* II, xxix–xxx, 225–37.

reality; the individual will not conform exactly to the rules, and the rules are not an exact measurement of the individual. This, if true in purely natural, human matters, is a hundred times more so when it is a question of God's dealing with the soul on a higher, spiritual level. There, our ignorance must always forbid us to claim omniscience and to speak dogmatically. Our knowledge, such as it is, must always be a compound of careful observation and theological principle.

The second and more important point is that theological principles, when once they are no longer the simple expression of clearly revealed truths, are inadequate expressions of the divine unity-in-multiplicity, of the infinitely free and flexible ways in which the Holy Spirit orders the disposal of his gifts and graces. Hence we must perpetually be on our guard to avoid both the Scylla of artificial, neat cataloguing and the Charybdis of vague and disordered narratives of experiences and feelings in which no distinction is made between the human and the divine.

Examples of the latter failing are legion; indeed, almost all popular treatment of mysticism is at fault, from William James to our own day. The principal instances of the former can be seen in those who follow without sufficient discernment what they take to be the teaching of St John of the Cross. Equating mysticism with contemplation, and contemplation with the dark experience of faith, and noting St John's ruthless dismissal of visions and locutions, they regard as inexplicable, or as positively non-significant, if not delusive, all the instances of divine communication with the soul that cannot be brought into line with their conception of pure contemplation, thereby dismissing a whole range of spiritual experience. It is true that St John and his followers appear at first sight to eliminate as worthless if not as harmful all that is not fully and purely supernatural, and by so doing they free souls and their directors from endless care and waste of time, but, if St John is regarded carefully, it will be seen that his methods are not so ruthless as they have been made to appear. He is presupposing a strong soul with an undoubted call to contemplation, and he proceeds by the most rapid way available to cut it off from all else. He does not deny the reality of the higher forms of vision or locution, but he emphasizes the dangers of pride and deception, and enumerates the principle that all such manifestations are merely the outward rind of a wholly invisible gift of grace which can be better received without the distraction of the mind and soul to superficial things.

St John, we must not forget, was not writing for the modern world of readers, nor for the large circle of mystical theologians of his contemporary Spain, nor even for any sort of publication, but for the friars and nuns of the infant Reform. There, and especially in the nunneries, there had been an almost Pentecostal effusion of graces, and the young sisters had before their eyes or in their hands on paper, the example of their Mother Foundress and her long history of visions and ecstasies. The spiritual and psychological climate of sixteenth-century Spain was charged with electricity of this sort, and St John, who was himself a figure of legend, may well have thought that a drastic re-orientation was necessary. Yet even so he is careful to safeguard the authenticity of some, at least, of these experiences, as also their value and moral necessity for some types of soul and stages of progress, and it seems clear that he would have admitted the possibility of the reception of even an intellectual vision by a soul outside the mystic way or in its lower stages. A more explicit assertion of the same judgement is made by St Teresa. Whether or not we allow the word "mystical" to be used of such experiences is largely a matter of the meaning we attach to the word. Theologians tend to assimilate such visions to the spiritual gift of "prophecy", but this in its primary meaning refers to a class of graces called *gratis datae*, graces, that is, bestowed primarily for the benefit of others than the recipient. The experiences we speak of would seem to border upon sanctifying grace and to prepare the soul for this Within this large category might come not only clear instances in the lives of the saints, but many of the well-known incidents that appear so often when mysticism is discussed, such as the Ostian conversation of Augustine and Monica and the midnight Fire of Blaise Pascal, and even some of the conversion narratives of the early Quakers and Methodists. If these graces are considered to be outside the specific category of sanctifying grace they would not presuppose a high degree of charity or any supernatural mystical receptivity in the recipient. The stimulus they give to the mind and will is not one of infused love and knowledge but of light, and in consequence love, flowing from a spiritual intuition which is neither wholly incommunicable nor merely formal and scientific.

St John of the Cross passes judgement on the whole class of "imaginary" visions and locutions:

> Since they are a means and manner whereby God guides such souls, there is no reason for thinking ill of them or for [the director] being alarmed and scandalized by them.... Let confessors direct their penitents into [the night of] faith, advising them frankly to turn away their eyes from all such things, teaching them how to void the desire and the spirit of them, so that they may make progress, and giving them to understand how much more precious in God's sight is one work or act of the will performed in charity than are all the visions and communications that they may receive from heaven, since these imply neither merit nor demerit. Let them point out, too, that many souls who have known nothing of such things have made incomparably greater progress than others who have received many of them.[2]

This clear statement offers an admirable summary of the question which we have been discussing and will serve as a conclusion to this chapter.

[2] *Ascent* II, xxii (Peers I, 173). This passage is sometimes cited to show that St John did not regard *mystical* experiences as sanctifying or meritorious, but he is not referring here to contemplation, but to locutions and revelations.

CHAPTER VII

MEDITATION AND CONTEMPLATION

During the past half-century the works of St John of the Cross, previously known only to theologians and a few of the contemplative Orders of religious, have attained a remarkable vogue in western Europe, with a circulation which would be large by any standards for a work of this kind. We are not here concerned to explain or to assess the value of this popularity, but rather to note that, as often happens when a book is read without any knowledge of its historical purpose or context, its statements, instructions and descriptions are frequently understood as applying to present-day situations and conditions altogether different from those which confronted the original author. This has certainly been the fate of the mystical writings of St John, and one point at least is so commonly and even excusably misunderstood that it may be well to mention it here.

This is the constant opposition between meditation and contemplation. St John throughout his writings uses these two terms not only as mutually exclusive (which they certainly are) but as if between them they covered the whole extent of the spiritual life, with the consequence that every devout person must in his prayer either meditate or contemplate. St John can even write such a sentence as "beginners ... pass from meditation to contemplation."[1] Such passages, not unnaturally, when read almost in isolation by one unfamiliar with the subject, have been applied almost literally to present-day situations. When meditation becomes distasteful or apparently impossible in a sincere and devout person it is assumed that what follows must be at least incipient contemplation. In consequence, discouragement and confusion may follow or (as is more common) the conception of contemplation is watered down to include not only the "prayer of simplicity", but even the most ordinary forms of simplified mental prayer.

In fact, as St John makes clear in many places, meditation is with him often shorthand for both explicit reflection and thought and all kinds of definite acts and conscious movements of the will in prayer, while contemplation includes both the first almost imperceptible infusion of the grace of recollection and the long periods of purifying aridity as well as mystical prayer in its fully formed and higher states. More important still, St John's whole corpus of instruction is given within the context of a very ascetic religious Order and is directed only to the more fervent members of that body. From these he could expect full spiritual understanding and rapid progress, but his teaching is only valid where like conditions are found.

St John opposes meditation to contemplation partly, no doubt, because, as we have already seen, contemplation, the specific and traditional occupation of the mystic, is formally a mental activity and thus demands by way of contrast another mental activity. But Christian contemplation has also, necessarily and even primarily, a volitional component; it is a matter of love as well as knowledge. Consequently the will and its love have an equal, nay a superior, place to the intellect and its knowledge in the mystical life, and it would in fact be

---

[1] *Living Flame* (1st redaction), stanza III, par. 30 (Peers III, 68); it may be noted that in the second redaction, stanza III, par. 32 (Peers III, 160) the phrase is omitted.

permissible to replace, or reduplicate, the "meditation-contemplation" antithesis with one (for which no proper technical terms exist) opposing the "forced" activity of human love in thought and word to the received energy of infused love. But partly because of this lack of appropriate terms, and partly because St John's masterpiece, *The Ascent of Mount Carmel*, breaks off unfinished without the promised chapters on the active night of the will, there is no direct and full treatment of the gradual change from active to fully supernatural love. As a result, meditation stands by itself in apparent isolation as the sole constituent of non-mystical prayer, whereas in fact "affective" prayer and "acts of the will" of love, acceptance, adoration and the like are as characteristic of the "state of beginners" as is meditation. Meditation, indeed, is not strictly speaking prayer at all, and the real correlative to contemplation is all prayer into which words, thoughts and active impulses of the will enter as the constituent element. Pure contemplative prayer is formless, infused love and knowledge; if it overflows into the normal faculties of the soul the words and feelings are its consequence, not itself. Consequently it would be altogether mistaken to suppose that by abandoning set meditation for affective prayer a person was passing from meditation to even the most embryonic form of contemplation. All that has happened is that the movements of love, adoration, sorrow and the rest, which are the essential parts of ordinary mental prayer, no longer need a formal mental framework to provide their motives, but are set in motion by the mere thought of God or of our Lord in his humanity or sacramental presence, and ultimately, as the prayer grows simpler, by an almost subconscious and habitual recognition of the presence of God. It is true that this prayer, which begins with the most rudimentary act that can fall under the definition of prayer, ends at the threshold of the prayer of simplicity beyond which comes, if indeed it ever comes, the beginning of infused contemplation. But meditation is strictly speaking no part of this prayer or, if we prefer to keep St John's word, it is a blanket term for the whole extent of non-mystical prayer.

Meditation, in the technical meaning it has borne since the fifteenth century, and which has been as it were canonized by the *Spiritual Exercises* of St Ignatius of Loyola, is really a miniature spiritual retreat with elements of instruction, pondering, praying and resolving. It was peculiarly suited to the mental climate of the sixteenth century, but it remains and will always remain a valid spiritual framework. For many, meditative reading will be an acceptable substitute for the introductory exercises of meditation, and may even, in the form of spiritual reading, be separated from the "affective" prayer which is its sequel. But formal meditation, however meritorious it may be as an exercise, is not prayer in the strict sense, but a preparation, a disposition, for prayer, and much confusion and embitterment and tilting at windmills might have been avoided had its advocates and critics alike recognized this. Those at least who use the word in the sense intended by St John of the Cross are fighting a wraith if they attack it.

St. John, indeed, is clearly and professedly addressing a very small class, the fervent leaven within a strict religious Order. He therefore hastens to higher things, touching briefly and selectively upon the lower stages. Often, without explicitly reminding us, he is assuming that he is addressing an Anne of Jesus or an Ana de Peñalosa. A Rubens is instructing a Vandyke. Where competence proceeds by steps, genius moves by flight. Consequently, we look in vain for a detailed instruction on the gradual progress of the normal devout religious from the first laborious meditations to a simpler, ever simpler form of prayer which may never, after decades of worthy observance, become mystical in any meaningful sense. Even when he is explicitly addressing "beginners" or their directors, the "beginners" are Carmelite friars and nuns of the the Reform who have shown at least the first signs of a fervent vocation.

CHAPTER VIII

THE DARK NIGHT

To many mysticism is a distasteful word. In part, no doubt, this is a justifiable reaction to the aberrations and morbidities which at one time or another have sheltered under its name, and also to the more authentic but entirely different psychological abnormalities that have appeared in the lives of some genuine mystics and have been misconceived as marvels. But quite apart from this, there is an element, perhaps there are two elements, in the lives of even the most balanced and humanly attractive of the mystics—a Francis, a Teresa, a Catherine of Siena—which repel many of those who approach with an initial sympathy. There is the element of darkness and the element of suffering.

The element of darkness is seen most strikingly in the phases in the mystical life which have been given the names of desolations and nights, and in the descriptions of those nights in the works of St John of the Cross, in whose classic presentation are summed up the less accurate sketches of medieval writers. The clarity of the mind's judgement seems to fade, and the life runs for a time, and perhaps for a long time, in a maze of doubt and uncertainty which to an observer and to a reader bear a strong superficial resemblance to the phases of psychological illness. It is one of the most notable of St John's achievements as a mystical theologian that he was able to explain what others had only described. The two nights, very different in their intensity, are not primarily evidences of physiological or psychological weakness, though they may contain an element of one of these; they are in essence the reaction of the powers of the soul, as yet weak and impure, to the superior light and love that is being poured into it, and that is experienced as darkness and aridity by the senses and by the mind. St John, in a vivid simile, compares this sense of instability and moral impurity to the blackening and exudates of a burning log under the influence of the flame that will in time render it incandescent.

The second element, that of suffering, is not so easily made acceptable to an age which has supped full of horrors, and endeavours to avoid, to hide and to forget every kind of physical suffering, an age which conceals the accompaniments of disease and death and drugs itself at the approach of physical pain and mental stress. A cultured and balanced scholar, an admirer of St Francis,[1] regarded his last months of physical suffering and mental distress as a sad exhibition of psychological failure under the strain of fighting for his ideals. Rather, it must be accepted that many of the physical catastrophes that beset the saints have an inestimable value not on account of pain stoically endured, but by reason of the love of God and men into which the suffering is converted. It must be accepted, also, that a Christian can follow his Master quite literally to the cross. It was St Paul, writing only thirty years and less after the historical fact of the crucifixion, who could write that he was nailed to the cross with Christ, that he bore the marks of Christ's ignominy in his body, that he filled up in his own body what was wanting to the sufferings of Christ, and many of the mystics have offered themselves, their lives and all they have to God on behalf of their fellow Christians and unbelievers, and their offering has been accepted. In this there is nothing morbid or unreal; it is an

---

[1] The late Professor F. C. Burkitt of Cambridge.

extension of the life of Christ in the members of his mystical body.

Even if the exact implication of these phrases of St Paul escapes us, we cannot suppose that the Apostle was using the language of rhetoric or exaggeration. In any case, mystics of all ages have lived those phrases in their fullest and deepest sense. They have prayed, with St Teresa, to suffer or to die for Christ; they have prayed with a full comprehension of what they were asking; and their prayer has been heard. They believed—and what Christian would dare to challenge the belief?—that all Christians may and should accept physical pain and mental anguish as a penalty and a purification of their faults, and that in a purified soul this may become a prolongation in the mystical body of Christ of the redemptive suffering of its Head, the greatest privilege given by the Redeemer of sharing his passion and giving themselves in love "for the remission of sins". Their action, like his, is visible only to the eyes of faith, known only to themselves and God.

Akin to this is the mysterious but real mental suffering which comes to the mystics in the meeting of their spirit with spiritual evil. In this they share in the suffering of their Lord in the garden of Gethsemane, in the hour of the lord of this world and of the power of darkness. St Teresa wrote: "I am well aware that the trials given by God to contemplatives are intolerable. ... I can assure you [her nuns] that you might not be able to endure their sufferings for as long as a day."[2]

In this love is the answer, and the only answer. Shakespeare, in his Desdemona, shows us a refinement and an admirable unselfishness in human love that surpasses normal experience. Human nature elevated by grace can attain a far deeper unselfishness. Faith and trust and love can inspire and demand the surrender of health and ease and life itself, and reach to the sharing of the cross of Christ and the dissolution of body

[2] *Way of Perfection*, XVIII (Peers II, 72-3).

and soul. The account to be given of the degrees of prayer may seem to be that of an introspective, narrow, egocentric life. These are indeed the faults which many, even devout Christians, think to see in contemplative religious, a desire to escape responsibility, a narcissus existence, given up to the pursuit and enjoyment of self-perfection. Nothing could be further from the truth. It is the fault of all abstraction and schematization that it regards only one aspect of its subject, and deprives even that of dimensions and depth. The infused love of contemplation is the love of God, which is inseparable, indeed identical in one sense, with the love of others. It is true that in its beginnings (beyond which many never pass) the love of God seems to be a negative force, rivalling and expelling what is commonly called love, but what is in reality either self-satisfaction or at best a movement towards a goodness and beauty infinitesimally small in comparison with the goodness of God, but in so far as the true, unselfish love of God increases under the influence of grace a truer and deeper love of others begins to dawn. The wholly unselfish, but also wholly personal love of the saints and mystics can be terrifying in its intensity, as that of Christ, who desired to cast fire upon the earth. We may almost think that a capacity for great love on the human level is a disposition, almost a condition *sine qua non*, for the reception of intense spiritual love. We may remember the parting of St Teresa of Avila from her father:

I remember—and I really believe this is true—that when I left my father's house my distress was so great that I do not think it will be greater when I die. It seemed to me as if every bone in my body were being wrenched asunder for, as I had no love of God to subdue my love for my father and kinsfolk, everything was such a strain for me that, if the Lord had not helped me, no reflection of my own would have sufficed to keep me true to my purpose.[3]

[3] *Life of St Teresa* IV (Peers I, 20).

We may remember also the agony of parting from her father endured by St Teresa of Lisieux, and compare these experiences with the abounding, unfailing and practical love poured out by these two saints in their different ways on all around them. It was St John of the Cross who wrote: "In the evening of life they will examine you in love",[4] and Sister Elizabeth of the Trinity who gave as her last message to her Carmelite sisters: "All passes away. In the evening of life only love remains. We must always forget ourselves."[5]

There is evidence enough in the lives of the mystics that the strictest personal austerity and dedication to God does not decrease, but increases to an immense extent the will and capacity to give to others, with absolute disregard of self. It was again St John who wrote to his nuns that they must give all their energies to the service of others, and end by giving themselves.[6]

[4] *Spiritual Sentences and Maxims* (Peers III, 225, n. 57): "a la tarde te examinarán en el amor."

[5] *Spiritual Doctrine of Sister Elizabeth of the Trinity* by M. M. Philipon, English translation (Cork, 1947), p. 31.

[6] *Spiritual Maxims* (Peers III, 225, n. 58): "Hasta que vienen a darse a si mismos."

CHAPTER IX

MYSTICISM AND DOGMA

The mystic's vision and the normal Christian adherence to precise dogma have often been contrasted or declared incompatible. The latter opinion is demonstrably false. The mystics belonging to denominations of dogmatic Christianity, and above all those of the Roman Catholic and Orthodox Churches, have been distinguished, almost without exception, by a lifelong adherence to the doctrines received in childhood. Moreover, of the few apparent exceptions who departed from common beliefs some, such as Eckhardt, held their unorthodox opinions (if indeed they had them) as philosophers or speculative theologians rather than as mystics.

More plausibly, it has been argued that mystics have interpreted Christian doctrines in an unusual or eccentric way, or at least that they have arrogated to themselves the gift of vision where others must be content with faith. Certainly, the true mystic receives knowledge which by definition is incommunicable because its content surpasses active reasoning, speaking or thinking. Whatever he puts into words is at best a translation, a paraphrase, of what he has seen; it may easily become a deformation or a parody. He is not concerned with formulating doctrines. What he has seen is in a sense supradogmatical. Garrulity, therefore, is a warning sign of falsehood in a mystic; a multitude of words or pictures must at the best contain a large element of natural, not to say egoistical, activity, and must therefore conceal, rather than reveal, whatever may have been received in the soul. It is rare that a visionary is able to find such lucid and deep expression of the truths of faith as does Dame Julian of Norwich, and even in her case to accept the words she attributes to our Lord or to God as being their authentic utterances is to misconceive the matter altogether. The words Dame Julian dictated were the best she could find to translate the ineffable, simple truths she had seen. A wordy mystic, or one who indulges in theological speculation, is no mystic.

Another charge that has been made against the mystical way is that in the outlook of the mystics the humanity of Christ, and indeed the whole dispensation of Incarnation and Redemption, and the deep Christian assurance of membership in the spiritual body of which Christ is head, are neglected or transcended. That such an opinion could ever be expressed in general terms can only be a result of the haphazard, purely empirical approach to the subject adopted by so many who have written of it. It is true, certainly, that nature-mystics and non-Christian mystics, of whom something will be said later, express the object of their love and worship in terms of monotheistic Divinity or even more simply in terms of supreme Spirit or transcendent Unity; for them the doctrines of the Incarnation and the Holy Trinity do not exist. It is true also, and this is a partial explanation of many misunderstandings, that the Christian mystical writers who were under the pervading influence of Neoplatonism, such as St Augustine, and in greater measure the pseudo-Denis and others, use Plotinian rather than evangelical or Pauline terms. Here each writer must be critically examined, and it will be found that many, as for example Augustine above all others, elsewhere in their writings proclaim Jesus Christ, the Word made Flesh, as the sole source of all spiritual gifts. Finally, among those who are at least nominally Christian and who claim some mystical experience, there have been a few examples of a non-Christian or a praeter-Christian approach. But when all these groups have been put aside, the great army of Christian mystics are unanimous in their assertion that it is through and in Christ that they attain to union with God and a knowledge of divine things. With many, this has never been called in question; if anything the emphasis they have laid on their union with Christ on the cross has obscured the theological depth of their insight, and the current term *Christocentric* has been opposed to that of *Theocentric*. It is therefore to this second so-called type (for among authentic Christians there is no essential division) that we must turn for the expression of what we have called the "universal" teaching. But first we may hear one of the earliest expositions of the doctrine, where John Cassian is reporting his interviews with the saints of the Egyptian desert. The Abbot Isaac is speaking:

> We shall never be able to accomplish that command [*sc.* to pray without ceasing] if our mind [which in Cassian's termi- nology denotes the soul] feeds not upon the unceasing con- templation of almighty God. This will be, when all our love, all our desire, all our study, all our effort, all our thought, all that we live and speak and breathe, becomes God, and when that eternal unity of Father and Son, Son and Father, is poured over into our senses and mind. That is to say, that as he loves us with simple, pure, and indissoluble love, so we may be joined inseparably to him in everlasting love, so that joined to him whatever we breathe or understand or speak may be God. Thus, I say, shall we attain the end which the Lord prayed might be accomplished in us: that "they all may be one as thou and I are one. I in them and thou in me, that they too may be perfected into one thing."[1]

Here, almost a thousand years later, is the author of *The Cloud of Unknowing* (*c.* 1370), who is often cited as a whole- hearted follower of the pseudo-Denis:

[1] Cassian, *Conferences*, Conference of Abbot Isaac, chapter X, quot- ing John 17. 2.

But whoso cometh not in by this way [sc. consideration of
the humanity of Christ] he cometh not truly; for he must stand
without and doth so, when he weeneth best he is within. For
many weeneth that they be within the ghostly door, and yet
stand they without, and shall do, unto the time that they seek
meekly the door. And some there be that find the door soon,
and cometh in sooner than some; and that is along of the
porter, plainly without price or deserving of themselves. . . .
For our Lord is not only porter himself, but also the door;
the porter by his Godhead and the door by his Manhood.
Thus saith he himself in the gospel: "I am the door".[2]

And here is St John of the Cross, whose teaching has been
likened, even by men of great learning, to that of the Buddhist
mystics:

He that would now inquire of God, or seek any vision or
revelation, would not only be acting foolishly, but would be
committing an offence against God, by not setting his eyes
altogether upon Christ, and seeking no new thing or aught
beside. And God might answer him after this manner, saying:
If I have spoken all things to thee in my Word, which is my
Son, and I have no other word, what answer can I now make
to thee, or what can I reveal to thee which is greater than
this? Set thine eyes on Him alone, for in Him I have spoken
and revealed to thee all things, and in Him thou shalt find
yet more than that which thou askest and desirest . . . He is
my complete locution and answer and He is all my vision and
all my revelation.[3]

And elsewhere he gives Christ as model for the ascetic and
as goal for the mystic life:

Have an habitual desire to imitate Jesus Christ in all His
actions, conforming yourself to His life (which must be carefully considered so as to know how to imitate it) and bearing
yourself in all things as He bore Himself.[4]

[2] *Epistle of Privy Counsel*, edited by Justin McCann, IX, pp. 218–19,
quoting John 10. 9.
[3] *Ascent* II, xxii (Peers I, 163).
[4] *Spiritual Maxims* (Peers III, 234 n. 2).

The Father spoke a single word; it was His Son, and He spoke it always in eternal silence and in silence must it be heard by the soul.[5]

More recently (1904) Sister Elizabeth of the Trinity, Carmelite of Dijon, wrote: "I have asked Him to take up His abode in me as Adorer, as Restorer, and as Saviour . . . He is there . . . to carry me further into Himself, into that divine Essence in which we already dwell by grace and in which I long to bury myself so deeply that nothing can ever draw me forth."[6] It is true that the mystic attains in the completeness of union to a knowledge in darkness of the Deity of the Holy Trinity rather than of the Persons of that Trinity, but this is precisely in virtue of his union with Christ, the Son of God, the Word. It is something altogether different from the philosopher's or the theologian's conception of the divine simplicity and unity.

[5] Ibid. (Peers 228, n. 21).
[6] *Spiritual Doctrine of Sister Elizabeth of the Trinity*, p. 117.

CHAPTER X

PRAYER

Prayer, the rising of the mind and heart to God,[1] the movement of adoration and love which is the first and last activity of all true religion, may seem at once too intimate and too simple to need or to be subjected to classifications and definitions. This is true, and at all times and in all places simple Christians have sought and found God, led only by their faith and by the Holy Spirit. St Benedict in his Rule gives in a phrase that has become celebrated the ultimate instruction: "If anyone wishes to pray, let him enter the oratory and pray in simplicity of heart."[2] Prayer is not a science or an exercise, but a turning of the whole being to God. No aid or intermediary is necessary, granted the aid of God who says to the soul, "I am here" before it calls upon him. In many regions and for many centuries Christians, and not they only, have prayed without rules and books.

Yet granted a complicated and literate society in which all read and are instructed, prayer, along with theology and every other form of human knowledge and activity, becomes a subject of instruction and observation and analysis, and its degrees and characteristics can be set down and may serve both to guide an individual and to display the sublimity of the

[1] The classic definition of prayer of St John Damascene is latinized by St Thomas Aquinas as *ascensus mentis in Deum*. Denis the Areopagite, also followed by St Thomas, defines prayer as "a giving and uniting of ourselves to God".

[2] *Rule of St Benedict*, ch. 52. *Simpliciter intret et oret.*

end to which all prayer tends. In what follows we mean by prayer the attempt of the soul to adore and to love God, approached either as the Deity or as one of the Divine Persons known by revelation. The prayer of asking or intercession is left aside, and the prayer of the heart is alone considered. The opposition of vocal and mental is inadequate; all true prayer is within the soul, deeper than words or thought. Vocal prayer is only true prayer when the heart and mind are praying, and the words may act as impulses to prayer, but to regard vocal prayer as a substitute for, or as an alternative to silent individual prayer, is to be wholly unrealistic, save in the case of the simple and of the contemplative. Love alone is the mainspring and the essence of prayer. *Ama, et fac quod vis.*

What may be called technical instruction on methods and degrees of prayer, as also the complementary ascetical teaching, is at least as old as the days of the Fathers of the Egyptian desert, and the Syrian and Cappadocian Fathers of the Church, and the principles they laid down have formed the basis, often unacknowledged, of all subsequent instruction. John Cassian in particular, whose writings summed up both the Egyptian and Syrian traditions, remained throughout the millennium that followed, from St Benedict to St Teresa, a *vade mecum* of the saints. His *Conferences* were read nightly in the monasteries of Europe for centuries; they were the daily reading of St Dominic and St Thomas Aquinas.

Nevertheless, from the days of Augustine to those of Aquinas prayer was rarely treated as a topic in isolation, and when it was touched upon it was merged in an abstract, theological consideration of all the powers of man, and at last became a small department of the vast scholastic catalogue of Christian duties and virtues. Saints and devout men and women prayed, as they may always do, with the personal instruction of an experienced spiritual guide, or led only by the Holy Spirit. What may be called detailed written instruction, or clear personal description, of higher forms of prayer is non-existent between St Gregory and St Bernard, one might almost say, between Cassian and Tauler. Contemplation was indeed discussed on the theological level, but in all the followers of St Augustine it is extremely difficult to disentangle theological and philosophical speculation from practical advice.

Direct instruction on contemplative prayer, as well as the description of individual experience, began in the Rhineland and South Germany with Tauler and Suso in the fourteenth century, and continued with Ruysbroeck and others in the Netherlands. At the same moment the group of English mystics were providing teaching that was closely parallel, but more clearly and orderly presented. Indeed, it may be said that the anonymous *Cloud of Unknowing* and the *Scale of Perfection* of Walter Hilton were the two first handbooks of contemplative prayer. They had no immediate successors in northern Europe, but their teaching reached Spain and influenced several, including the greatest, of the multitude of spiritual writers who appeared there in the sixteenth century. Among and above these rose the two Carmelite saints, St Teresa of Avila and St John of the Cross. It is sometimes regretted that these two are quoted so universally, but it must be admitted as inevitable. Not only do they stand in the full stream of tradition that flowed from France and northern Europe, but they are so copious and exhaustive in their writings, so pre-eminent in their sureness of doctrine and wealth of experience, so striking and so complementary in their personality and style that no single writer, or group of writers, can challenge them as rivals. The great names of the generations that followed, St Francis de Sales, Fr Augustine Baker, Abbot Blosius, Benet of Canfield, Constantine Barbanson, Lallemant and the rest either follow their teaching in essentials or are, taken singly, narrower in scope or less clear in their teaching. While an exclusive or blind adherence

to any master save Christ is most undesirable, we cannot fail
to recognize that no mystical writer since their day has combined breadth and precision, doctrinal purity and personal
authority in any comparable degree. In the centuries that have
passed since their day numberless contemplatives and theologians have endorsed their teaching. In what follows, therefore, they will be given pride of place, and the Englishman
Walter Hilton will be cited as a representative of tradition
two centuries earlier.

Two words of caution may precede the survey of mystical
prayer. The one is, that prayer cannot, and must not, be
isolated in the Christian life, as if it alone were the way of
life. Yet at the same time advancement in the spiritual following of Christ and in the love of God are intimately and in-
extricably bound together by prayer. If, as is surely the truth,
prayer increases in purity as the love, hope and faith of the
soul increase, and if, as has been accepted on an earlier page,
growth in charity and sanctity is, or should be, a progress
unbroken by sudden or accidental changes, the traditional map
of prayer may be accepted as showing an aspect of the whole
spiritual life. In that map prayer is seen as becoming gradually
less and less a matter of words or motions of the will and
more and more a simple loving attention to God, until this
too merges into a new realization or experience of the presence
of God in the soul, with its accompaniment of a new knowledge and love of God which do not come from any purely
human thought or motion. Herein is the beginning of the
mystical life. The eloquent and moving words of St Teresa
are well known:

> Herein [i.e., in mental prayer] there is nothing to be afraid
> of, but everything to hope for ... for mental prayer is nothing
> else, in my opinion, but being on terms of friendship with God.
> ... I have seen this distinctly in my own case, and I cannot
> tell why the whole world does not labour to draw near to Thee
> in this particular friendship ... only this will I say: prayer is

the door to those great graces which our Lord bestowed on me. If this door be shut, I do not see how he can bestow them.[3]

The first counsel of all the masters is for a firm resolve. In his parable of the pilgrim to Jerusalem, the city of peace, which is contemplation, Walter Hilton exhorts:

> Do not stop for anything that you hear or see or feel. Make no pause for it, do not look at it, do not take pleasure in it, do not fear it. Keep on your way and have no aim but to be at Jerusalem, for that is what you desire, and nothing but that.[4]

St Teresa uses almost the same words:

> How must one begin? I maintain that this is the chief point; in fact that everything depends on their having a great and most resolute determination never to halt until they reach their journey's end, happen what may, whatever the consequences are, cost what it will, let who will blame them, whether they reach the goal, or die on the road, or lose heart to bear the trials they encounter, or the earth itself goes to pieces beneath their feet.[5]

Neither Walter Hilton nor St John of the Cross set out in order the normal progress of the soul in prayer. For that we must turn to St Teresa who, with all her diffuseness and repetitions and minor inconsistencies, must remain the supreme mistress of sensitive, experiential and psychologically true analysis, based on her own experience and her observation of others. In the *Life* her account is dominated by her celebrated simile drawn from the various methods of watering a garden— by water drawn from a well, by that drawn by an engine and buckets (the Spanish *noria*), by a stream, and by showers of rain. Here we are concerned only with the two first methods. The water drawn from the well is the laborious recollection of mind of "those who are beginners in prayer", who "must

---

[3] *Life*, viii (Peers, I 50).
[4] *Scale of Perfection*, II xxi 192ff.
[5] *Way of Perfection*, xxi (Peers, II 89).

strive to meditate on the life of Christ". Meditation, in her context, would include the affective acts and resolutions that form part of every set exercise of prayer. After describing the state of dryness and distractions that overtakes many in this prayer she proceeds to give her first sketch of the prayer which she continued to the end of her life to consider the best disposition for further progress. As it is in some ways her most distinctive contribution to the analysis of the development of the life of grace, and as it has been the object of considerable discussion and misunderstanding, it will be well to scrutinize it carefully at its first appearance. We must be clear at the outset that this prayer is not "infused" or "supernatural". St Teresa, as we shall see, expressly asserts this, and indeed her whole description of this prayer occurs in the chapters devoted to the first degree or method of raising water from the well.

> The soul [she writes] may ... place itself in the presence of Christ ... this is a most safe way of advancing in the first state of prayer and of attaining quickly to the second. ... This then is what we can do. He who would pass out of this state and upraise his spirit to experiences that are denied to him will, in my opinion, lose both one and the other [i.e., lose the advertence of faith to the presence of Christ and fail to attain to "infused" sense of his presence].[6]

In *The Way of Perfection*, written a few years after the *Life*, she describes this prayer once more, now calling it "the prayer of recollection":

> You know that God is everywhere ... we need no wings to go in search of Him but have only to find a place where we can be alone and look upon Him present within us ... this is a prayer that brings with it many blessings. It is called recollection because the soul collects together all the faculties and enters within itself to be with its God. ... Those who are thus

[6] *Life*, xii (Peers, I 71–2).

able to enclose themselves within this little heaven of the soul
... may be sure that they are travelling by an excellent way....
In the beginning it requires a painful effort, for the body claims
its rights ... but by persevering in the habit for several days,
and by controlling ourselves, the benefits that result will become
clear.... I advise whoever wishes to acquire this habit, which,
as I said, we have it in our power to gain, not to grow tired
of persevering in trying gradually to obtain the mastery of
herself.... Nothing can be learnt without a certain amount of
trouble. For the love of God, sisters, reckon your time well
spent in acquiring this habit. I know that, with His help, if
you practise it for a year, or perhaps only for six months, you
will gain it. You must understand that this is not something
supernatural, but something which, with the grace of God, we
can desire and obtain for ourselves.[7]

These passages of St Teresa, clear as they are, need a commentary. In the first place, it is clear that the prayer she is
describing is not mystical. She insists on telling us this, by
repeating that it is not "supernatural". Strictly speaking, any
act of faith or love of God in a Christian is "supernatural",
that is, it is made possible, inspired, and assisted by grace.
But by supernatural St Teresa here means prayer that requires
a grace higher than that upon which every Christian may rely,
an enablement that is doubly supernatural, that is, not only
in itself, essentially, but by reason of the way in which it acts,
by the direct "infusion" of knowledge and love.

Next, it must be remembered that St Teresa is writing for
Carmelite nuns who have proved their ability to live a life
of hardship, enclosure and psychological solitude. What is
possible for such is not possible for all devout persons, for
there is no "flat rate" of grace. Only the individual, wisely
counselled, can judge whether this prayer, "active" though it
be, is the prayer to which God is enabling him. It is the prayer
to which Bossuet, in the last years of his life, called the nuns

[7] *Way of Perfection*, xxviii–xxix (Peers, I 114–122).

of whom he was the superior. He will scarcely be suspected of Quietism:

> We must acquire the habit of strengthening the soul by a simple and loving look upon God and our Lord Jesus Christ, and for this purpose we should wean it gently from reasoning, from discursive thought and from a multitude of affective acts, and maintain a simple and reverent attention while we approach nearer and nearer to God, our only sovereign good.
> ... The practice of this prayer should begin by an act of faith in the presence of God, who is in all places, and of Jesus Christ, whose gaze is upon us even if we were buried at the centre of the earth. This act of faith is made either as one might say within oneself: "I believe that my God is present", or as a purer and more spiritual recollection by faith of the presence of God.[8]

And St John of the Cross: "Enter into your heart and labour in the presence of God who is always present there to help you. Fix your loving attention upon Him without any desire to feel or hear anything of God."[9]

There has been a great deal of writing about this kind of prayer in the past fifty years. All that need be said here is to make it clear that it is not mystical prayer or "contemplation" in any traditional sense of that word, but on the other hand that it is a stage or degree of prayer which cannot be exercised, and should not be recommended, indiscriminately. To many it has neither meaning nor attraction. Others will feel it to be familiar and as it were natural and satisfying. *Qui potest capere capiat.*

---

[8] Bossuet, *Manière courte et facile pour faire l'oraison en foi et de simple présence de Dieu* (*Œuvres*, Paris (1840), IV 610). This opuscule is included in the works of Bossuet, and has never formally been challenged. My personal opinion is that the Bossuet who wrote *Sur les états d'oraison* could never have written this excellent, though theologically imprecise, little treatise.

[9] *Spiritual Maxims* (Peers III 227 nos. 11, 4).

Above this, in so far as a line can be drawn, the first light of the mystical life begins to appear. But before looking at it we may hear St Teresa again:

> He who would pass out of this state and raise his spirit to experiences that are denied to him will, in my opinion, lose both one and the other [i.e., lose the advertence of faith to the presence of God and fail to attain to the "infused" sense of his presence] since this [i.e. the experiential knowledge] is supernatural; and if the understanding ceases the soul finds itself desolate and in great dryness. What I am saying—namely, let them not rise if God does not raise them—is the language of spirituality. He will understand me who has had any experience. ... In mystical theology [i.e. infused contemplation] the understanding ceases from its acts, because God suspends it. ... We must neither imagine nor think that we can bring about this suspension. That is what I say must not be done. Nor must we cause the understanding to cease from its acts, for in that case we shall be stupid and cold, and the result will be neither the one nor the other. For when our Lord suspends the understanding, and makes it cease from its acts, He puts before it that which holds its attention and occupies it. ... Again I repeat my advice; it is of great moment not to raise our spirit ourselves, if our Lord does not raise it for us; and if He does, there can be no mistaking it.[10]

This long extract shows St Teresa at her best. The reader will surely feel that the danger of Quietism has never been defined more wisely, save perhaps by St John of the Cross, who uses almost the same words in a passage less familiar than that of St Teresa:

> If the soul at that time had not this [infused] knowledge of God or this realization of His presence, the result would be that it would do nothing and have nothing; for having turned aside from meditation and being still without contemplation, ... the soul would of necessity be without any exercise in the

[10] *Way of Perfection*, xii (Peers, II 72).

things of God either by working with the faculties of sense or receiving with the faculties of spirit.[11]

St Teresa ends her account of this prayer with the words: "I have dwelt so long upon this matter because this way of prayer is the most common with beginners."[12] The last word must not deceive us, as it has deceived many in the pages of St John of the Cross. In the traditional spiritual life, the beginner is opposed to the progressive or proficient who is already in the first stages of the mystical life. One who considers the Christian life in its fullness must not lower his sights. In the spiritual life, as in every art and science, the majority remain beginners for the whole of life.

This prayer, which St Teresa describes, is, it need scarcely be said, not an invention on her part. Writing at the beginning of the great modern age of analysis she was the first to put her experience and observation into words. From her day to the present it has been regarded as a normal degree of prayer for truly devout souls, and although it is not mentioned by name by St John of the Cross, the prayer is described by him and we know that he recommended it to the young friars and nuns under his direction. It soon came to bear the name of "acquired contemplation", and in after times a misconceived image of it was inflated to cover the lower stages of truly mystical prayer, while the term "infused contemplation" was reserved for the higher (and therefore far rarer) mystical experiences. Space need not be used here to eliminate such opinions. Common experience suffices, and we have already quoted the explicit assertion of St Teresa. Her prayer of recollection is not mystical, and it differs specifically from mystical contemplation.

At the same time we must not make the opposite mistake of conceiving the degrees of the spiritual life as terraces rising above each other in lofty precipices. Spiritual, like natural,

11 *Ascent of Mount Carmel*, II xiv (Peers, I 113–14).
12 *Way of Perfection*, xii (Peers, II 73).

growth is normally gradual, if it continues, and comes like the dawn of day. We can recognize the darkness of night and the rays of the sun, but who can say when night passes into day? Objects loom up, trees can be identified, colour begins to show, yet it is still not light enough to read. It is for this reason that mistakes can so easily be made over this degree of prayer. As it is the lowest step above "meditation" it is the broadest and has innumerable degrees of purity. But when all is said and done it is a recognizable stage. It is not mystical prayer, and any classification of it as contemplation is misleading, and those who practise it are not contemplatives in any meaningful theological sense of the word. On the other hand, it is recognizable as a real stage in the spiritual life. The assertion of St Teresa that it can be acquired must not be taken to mean that, like bicycling or swimming, it merely needs a short instruction and some practice. St Teresa may have misled some by her somewhat offhand empirical assertion that it can be acquired in a year or six months. We may forget that she herself spent fifteen years when prayer was tedious to her and that she has already described at some length the first stage of prayer, its difficulties and its distractions, the need for a serious resolve and the absolute sacrifice of all else save God. Those who have in truth made that sacrifice will need no instruction in this prayer.

It is only when the prayer of recollection has become settled and pure, maintained through aridities and distractions for long, that it can be regarded as in any sense a disposition for infused contemplation. When St Teresa begins "to speak of the beginning of pure contemplation, which is called the prayer of quiet,"[13] her language is utterly different:

> This prayer [she writes] is something supernatural to which no effort of our own can raise us, because here the soul rests in peace—or rather, our Lord gives it peace by his presence.[14]

[13] *Ibid.* (Peers, II 125).
[14] *Ibid.*, xxxi (Peers, II 127).

And again:

> We cannot make the day break, nor can we stop night from coming on. This prayer is no work of ours: it is supernatural and utterly beyond our control. The surest way to prolong it is to recognize that we can neither diminish nor add to it, and, unworthy as we are, we can but receive this grace with thanksgiving.

While giving to it the generic and already conventional name of the "prayer of quiet" she makes it clear that it has several degrees, or rather a gradual growth in purity:

> The first prayer which I experienced which seems to me supernatural I should describe as one which, despite all our efforts, cannot be acquired by industry or diligence.... This prayer is an interior recollection felt in the soul, which seems to have acquired new senses, corresponding to its exterior senses.... In this prayer there is no loss of any of the senses or faculties, which are still fully active; but their activity is concentrated upon God. This will be easily understood by anyone to whom our Lord has granted it, but anyone else cannot fail to need a great many words and comparisons.[16]

She continues:

> From this prayer there usually comes what is called a sleep of the faculties; these, however, are not so completely absorbed and suspended that it can be called a rapture.[17]

And she adds, as elsewhere:

> Sometimes, often indeed, the soul is aware that the will alone is in union, and this it understands very clearly.... The will is wholly concentrated upon God ... but its other two faculties are free to act and work in God's service.[18]

And again:

> The powers of the soul are at peace ... but they are not so lost, for they can realize in Whose presence they are, Who has

[15] *Ibid.* (Peers II 129).
[16] *Relation V* (ed. Lewis-Zimmerman Relation VIII), Peers I 327.
[17] *Ibid.*, 328.   [18] *Ibid.*

made them free. The will alone is captive.... The understanding centres itself on one thing only, and the memory tries to occupy itself with nothing else, for they see that this is "the one thing needful" and that anything else disturbs them.[19]

And:

The soul is here like a babe at the breast of its mother, who to refresh it drops the milk into its mouth when it makes no attempt to suck. Thus it is now, for the will loves without any use of the understanding.... Any effort made to constrain the understanding to take part in what is passing will result in failure; being forced it will cause the milk to fall from its mouth.... what I say is important, although it may seem only jargon. In this state the mind disturbs the soul, which is not the case when there is union of the three faculties.[20]

In another place, still more vividly:

Let us imagine that the powers of the soul... have fled and joined the enemy [outside the "interior castle" of the soul]. After long days and years of absence, perceiving how great has been their loss, they return to the neighbourhood of the castle, but cannot manage to re-enter it.... The King [God] sees their good will... and out of His great mercy desires them to return to Him. Like a good shepherd, with a piping so sweet that even they themselves scarce hear it, He makes them recognize His voice and no longer wander like lost sheep, but return to their mansion.[21]

And once more she reiterates that it is "supernatural" prayer:

Do not fancy that it can be acquired by the understanding, by thinking of God dwelling within you, or by the imagination, imagining Him in your soul: this is a good practice, and an excellent kind of meditation.... but it is not this [recollection], for by the divine assistance everyone can practise that [i.e.,

[19] *Way of Perfection*, xxxi (Peers, II 128).
[20] *Ibid.* (Peers, II 131).
[21] *Interior Castle*, IV iii (Peers, II 240).

meditation on the presence of God], but what I mean is quite a different thing.[22]

And she insists:

I think I read somewhere that the soul then behaves itself like a tortoise or sea-urchin, which retreats into itself. He who wrote this doubtless understood it in the right way; but these creatures can withdraw themselves at will, while here it is not in our power to retire into ourselves, unless God gives us the grace.[23]

This prayer of "supernatural" recollection is followed by what St Teresa calls the "prayer of Quiet", using what is the generic name of the several degrees of increasing absorption of the faculties for what is the most complete, short of "union".

This is a supernatural state, and, however hard we try, we cannot reach it for ourselves.... The soul, in a way which has nothing to do with the outward senses, realizes that it is now very close to its God, and that, if it were but a little closer, it would become one with Him through union.[24]

Gradually the other faculties besides the will become captive:

This state is a sleep of the faculties, which are neither wholly lost nor yet can understand how they work.... this kind of prayer, I think, is quite definitely a union of the entire soul with God, except that His Majesty appears to be willing to give the faculties leave to understand and have fruition of the great things that He is now doing.[25]

From this point onwards it becomes increasingly difficult to give a clear account of the further degrees of prayer in St Teresa's own words, partly, and essentially, because the unfamiliarity and incommunicability of the experience become complete, but partly, also, because St Teresa, in the three

[22] *Ibid.* (Peers, II 241).
[23] *Ibid.* The writer referred to is Osuna, *Third Spiritual Alphabet*, VI iv.
[24] *Way of Perfection*, xxxi (Peers, II 127).
[25] *Life*, xvii (Peers, I 102).

books in which she gives her account, becomes at this point
diffuse and repetitive, and devotes far more space and attention to describing the accidental circumstances—raptures,
visions, locutions and the like—than she gives to the essence
of the mystical experience. With care and patience, however,
it is possible to follow her through the first prayer of union
to the fuller union which in her case was accompanied by the
psycho-physical condition which she calls ecstasy and thence
to the spiritual betrothal and spiritual marriage. Despite the
apparently personal and superficial detail and many irrele-
vancies, the thread of ever-growing purity of soul and ever-
increasing capacity for bearing every kind of physical and
mental suffering is never lost, and readers will not fail to note
that the sense of loss of God and of any faith or love or
experience of any spiritual reality whatever occur after the
spiritual betrothal, at the point where St John of the Cross
begins his account of the summits of the mystical way in the
Spiritual Canticle with the stanza *Dove te ascondisti* ("Whither
hast thou vanished?"). It is only too easy to feel distaste or
simply mystification in the fluidity and deceptively simple and
superficial descriptions of St Teresa, and to miss the hard core
of spiritual doctrine and strength. It may be well to end this
brief exposition of her spiritual pilgrimage with her sober
phrases on the spiritual marriage:

There is the same difference between the spiritual betrothal
and the spiritual marriage as there is between two betrothed
persons and two who are united so that they cannot be separated any more. As I have already said, one makes these
comparisons because there are no other appropriate ones, yet
it must be realized that the betrothal has no more to do with
the body than if the soul were not in the body, and were
nothing but spirit. Between the spiritual marriage and the body
there is even less connection, for this secret union takes place
in the deepest centre of the soul, which must be where God
Himself dwells, and I do not think there is any need of a door

by which to enter it. . . . It is impossible to say more than that, as far as one can understand, the soul is made one with God who, being likewise a Spirit, has been pleased to reveal the love that He has for us by showing to certain persons the extent of that love, so that we may praise His greatness. For He has been pleased to unite Himself with His creature in such a way that they have become like two who cannot be separated from one another. . . . It is as if a tiny streamlet enters the sea, from which it will find no way of separating itself. . . . Perhaps when St Paul says "He who is joined to God becomes one spirit with Him", he is referring to this sovereign marriage, which presupposes the entrance of His Majesty into the soul by union. And he also says: *Mihi vivere Christus est, mori lucrum.* This, I think, the soul may say here, for it is here that the little butterfly to which we have referred dies, and with the greatest joy, because Christ is now its life.[26]

St Teresa, as has been said, tells of the life of the spirit by way of external, personal details, largely drawn from her own experience. Nevertheless, the sharp lines of psychological and theological reality lie behind her words. St John of the Cross proceeds, at least in the eyes of many who read him, by way of theological principles and detailed analysis, without any account of personal experience, though it is clear that his firm and authoritative assertions can rest upon nothing that has not been seen and experienced.

St John says little of methods and degrees of prayer. His teaching rests upon the twofold approach to God, that is, the certainty that he cannot be known as he is by any human power or faculty, but that by the supernatural gifts of faith and love his transcendence of all that can be known or imagined can become progressively clear; while as a consequence of the elimination of all other objects of love God himself may by his infused love turn all the powers of the soul to himself. St John's division of the mystical way into

---

[26] *Interior Castle*, VII ii (Peers, II 334–5).

the twofold night of sense and spirit, each considered in an active and a passive, a human and a divine interaction, is well known, but it is not so well known that he was following and developing a traditional path of spirituality. The following passage of Walter Hilton might well be taken from *The Ascent of Mount Carmel*:

> The man who perceives that the love of this world is false and does not last, and for this reason wishes to forsake it and seek the love of God, cannot immediately experience his love, but must stay for a time in the night.... This night consists in nothing else than a withdrawal of the soul from the things of earth by a great desire and longing to love and see and experience Jesus [the divine Person] and spiritual things. This is the night; for just as the night is dark and material objects are hidden in it ... so a man who determines to fix his mind on Jesus and to desire only his love, must give neither his thoughts nor his love to bodily creatures.... If he can do this, he is in the night, for he is in darkness.... This night is distressing at first ... nevertheless if you find it so ... be patient and ... if you can, quietly turn your will and your thought to Jesus ... your soul by grace will become so free and strong, and so recollected, that it will find no attraction in earthly thoughts, and no material thing will prevent it from thinking of something above it that it does not know and does not yet possess, but which it desires and yearns after eagerly.[27]

The teaching of St John in barest outline rests upon two commonplaces of Christian doctrine: that human nature in general and in the individual is weakened and blinded by original and personal sin in the form of self-love and self-indulgence; and that a soul can be healed of these failings through the grace of God by faith and love, and so attain even

---

[27] *Scale of Perfection*, II xxiv 205–6. Hilton's use of "Jesus", when we would expect "God" or "the Word" has caused difficulty to some readers. It has been suggested that the Holy Name was substituted for "God" by a pietistic scribe. Perhaps the long-awaited critical edition will give some information on the point.

on earth to a union of will with Christ the Son of God. The
two enemies, the two obstacles, to this are the love of any
person or thing regarded as apart from God, and the mistaking
of any creature or created knowledge or idea for God. To
vanquish or to escape from these two dangers or enemies,
which can in some sense be regarded as successive, because
the second does not become fully apparent till the first has
been at least in part vanquished, two processes are necessary.
The one is the active direction or withdrawal of the powers
from selfish or sense-gratifying desires by rational "ascetic"
action assisted by grace; the other is the inpouring of light
and strength within the faculties themselves. Both these processes are active in themselves and in the soul, but in the
former the powers of the individual are directed and moved
by the reason and will, assisted imperceptibly by grace, in the
latter they are moved, freely, vitally and efficaciously, by the
grace of God to which they consent and to which they give
way without hindrance. From the point of view of the human
being, therefore, these two processes may be distinguished as
active and passive, with the proviso that passivity here does
not imply the cessation or negation of human activity, but
the assumption of the lower, human, activity into the higher
activity of God.

There are thus in St John's scheme two nights (or escapes)
of sense and of spirit, each of which can be divided into two
parts or levels—active and passive, ascetical and mystical. As
the names suggest, the active nights can be entered at will
(with the inspiration and enablement of grace), while the
passive nights lie entirely beyond man's endeavour. As it is
also St John's repeated teaching that complete freedom from
the desires of the senses can only result from divine purifying
action in the passive night of sense, it must follow logically
that the active night of the spirit takes place after the passive
night of sense, upon which it depends for its preparation, and
as this latter is of its nature a mystical purification, the active

as well as the passive night of the spirit falls within the mystical way. Such was no doubt schematically St John's conviction, but it must never be forgotten that he reminds us constantly that souls differ greatly in their qualities, gifts and graces. Within a group of individuals the strength of endeavour, the severity of purification and the abundance of grace vary to an indefinite degree, and it is doubtless possible that the active, ascetic night of the spirit might begin before the passive night of sense had been completed. It is also true that the night of sense is "common", whereas the night of spirit is rare. In other words, there may be a rudimentary "mystical" life for many, though St John would probably prefer to say that the passive night of sense is often only a faint foreshadowing of the intense night of the spirit.

Readers of St John and commentators upon him are prone to forget that in order to make his teaching both clear and all-embracing he is primarily interested in setting out the career of a soul richly endowed by nature and grace, and corresponding to the enablements it receives in order to attain to the highest state possible in this life. Those who look carefully, not only at his treatises, but at his letters also and his counsels, will see that he was well aware that in the concrete case all kinds of difference and deviation would occur, and that many a devout individual might spend a lifetime neither fully in, nor fully outside, one or other of the nights.

Throughout the writings of St John there run two basic theological conceptions which are certainly not of his invention, but which he seizes and develops more insistently than most of his predecessors. There is, first, the constant teaching that neither God himself nor any divine attribute or action—nothing, in short, that is strictly supernatural—can be perceived or received in its own nature by the senses or natural intellectual powers of man. On the other hand, the Christian, when called and enabled and purified by God, can receive an objective knowledge of God which is not indeed the vision reserved for the souls of the blessed, but is a supernatural knowledge flowing from an infused and wholly supernatural love of God which gives to the soul a knowledge of God by way of resemblance and sympathy which is at the same time accompanied by an infused, obscure knowledge of the absolute transcendence of God above and beyond any idea or intuition that the human mind can frame. In the words of St Thomas: "We know God by means of not knowing him, and by means of a union with him above all capacity of the human mind . . . and knowing him thus, the mind is enlightened from the very depths of divine wisdom, which we cannot pierce with our knowledge."[28] This is the true and full mystical union, with which visions and ecstasies, thoughts and descriptions, have nothing to do.

The second postulate is that within the mystical way all that can be clearly felt or known or expressed of the divine action upon the soul is the translation, sometimes faulty, always inadequate, of the infused light and love by the natural faculties of the soul. Thus the darkness and anxieties of the two nights are (in so far as they are genuinely part of the mystical way) the pain of the natural faculties in the presence of infinite love and utter simplicity which exceed altogether their range of perception. To a soul which is still selfish and merely human the demands and the abandonment of divine love are unbearable; to the mind a glimpse of divine light, whether it shows the nothingness of creatures or the transcendence of God, blinds and sears the intellect. Dark "contemplation" and the unfelt love of what is seen by faith alone are thus of themselves not trials or aridities sent by God, but the effect of infused love and truth upon imperfect and narrow powers of reception.

St John, as has been said, is not concerned with the degrees of prayer, either as matter of practical direction or as a thermometer of growth. His own story of the progress of his

[28] *Commentary on the Divine Names of Denis*, ch. vii 4.

soul, so far as he gave a thought to it, is told in his three great poems. In his treatises he is analytical, speaking in terms of faculties and powers, not of the fortunes of an individual. When asked, as no doubt he was often asked by his novices, how to pray, we can imagine him answering that to pray is to love, and that to talk of ways of prayer to one who does not love is to teach painting to the blind. Indeed, as he begins his teaching at the moment when "meditation" is ceasing and "contemplation" beginning, there is room only for the prayer we have seen St Teresa discussing so often and at such length, the prayer of recollection which passes (if indeed it ever changes) from active to contemplative prayer almost unperceived. In his own words: "We must know that the state and exercise of beginners is one of meditation and of the making of discursive exercises and acts with the imagination. In this state, it is necessary for the soul to be given material for meditation and reasoning, and it is well for it to make interior acts on its own account."[29]

But when the soul has "acquired fortitude and constancy" meditation and discursive acts begin to cease and, if the soul is truly sincere and strong, the three signs show that it should abandon meditation. St John describes the psychological reason for this:

> The end of reasoning and meditation on the things of God is the gaining of some knowledge and love of God, and each time that the soul gains this through meditation it is an act; and just as many acts of whatever kind end in forming a habit in the soul, just so, many of the acts of loving knowledge which the soul has been making one after another from time to time come through repetition to be so continuous in it that they become habitual. And thus that which aforetime the soul was gaining gradually through its labour of meditation upon particular facts has now through practice, as we have been saying, become converted into a habit and substance of loving

[29] *Living Flame,* III par. 32 (Peers, III 159–60).

knowledge of a general kind. . . . Wherefore, when it gives itself to prayer, the soul is now like one to whom water is brought, so that he drinks peacefully, without labour.[30]

And the soul has then to walk with loving advertence to God, without making specific acts but conducting itself, as we have said, passively [i.e., without distinct thoughts or acts] and making no efforts of its own, but preserving this simple, pure and loving advertence and determination, like one who opens his eyes with the advertence of love.[31]

In the last lines St John has passed into the cloud of unknowing. Both he and St Teresa, and indeed all those who describe the stages of the mystical way, cease from a clear and ordered account on the threshold of the prayer of union. Looking from below and from without we may see many reasons for this. With the prayer of union the last trace of thought or of humanly exercised love ceases and the ineffable enters in; the purely supernatural work of the Holy Spirit increases and becomes at once more obscure and more individual. Mystics, among whom Hilton is not the first and St John is not the last, love to speak of the hidden manna and the new name of the Apocalypse, that no man knows but he who receives it. All we can say, following in part the descriptions of the mystics and in part the line of advance that goes from the many to the one, from the clear to the obscure, from the imperfect to the perfect simplicity, is to record that the passing experiences of union culminate in a perfection which has come to be called the mystical espousal, in which the soul sees an earnest of the lasting presence of the Beloved, but can experience only passing visits. St Bernard is one of the earliest to speak of this in detail, and his account, eloquent if somewhat rhetorical as is all Bernard's speech, may be glanced at here: He is speaking to his monks in

[30] *Mount Carmel*, II xiv (Peers, I 111–2).
[31] *Living Flame*, III par. 32 (Peers, III 159–60).

chapter, but his words have been, as it were, revised for publication:

> And now bear with my foolishness a little. I wish to tell you, as I have promised, how it is with me in these matters. It is not expedient, indeed, but I will betray myself that I may benefit you, and if it helps you I shall be consoled for my foolishness; if not, I will freely confess it. I confess that even to me the Word has come—I speak as one less wise—and that many times. And though he often came to me, I always failed to mark his coming. I realized that he was there: I remembered that he had been. Sometimes, I could have a presentiment of his coming, but I could never perceive either his coming or his going. Whence he came into my soul or whither he went when he left me, and how he entered or departed I confess I am ignorant to this day, as it is written: "thou knowest not whence he comes or whither he goes". . . . Can it be that he did not enter, because he did not come from without? Nor is he any part of the universe around us. Neither does he come from within, since he is good and I know there is no good in me. You ask how then I know him to be present, if it be so that all his ways are unsearchable? He lives and works, and as soon as he came within me he aroused my drowsy soul; he moved, he softened, he wounded my heart, when it was hard and stony and sick. He began also to pluck up and destroy, to build and to plant, to water what is dry, to enlighten what is dark, to open what is closed, to inflame what is frozen, to make crooked ways straight and rough ways smooth, that my soul might bless the Lord and all that is within me praise his holy name. Thus often the Word, the Spouse, entering within me made his coming known by no sign at all; neither by word, nor appearance, nor step. I recognized him by no movement of his, by no sense-perception of mine, when he entered my inmost being. Only by the movement of my heart, as I have said, did I recognize his presence, and by the vanishing of my vices and the restraint of human affections did I note his power. . . . But when the Word departed from me all these blessings began to droop with cold and fatigue just as if you had withdrawn the fire from under a boiling pot. This for me is the sign of his

departure, that my soul must needs be sad until he come again, and my heart grow warm again within me as it does, and this is the sign of his return. Having such experience of the Word what wonder is it if I too make use of the word of the Betrothed in recalling him when he absents himself, for I too am carried away by a longing not equal but like in part to hers. As long as I live the word of recall, recalling the Word, will be always in my heart, the word "Return". And as often as he vanishes I will repeat it, and I will not cease to cry, as it were crying after one departing, with burning longing that he should return, and give back to me the joy of my salvation, give back to me himself. I say to you, my sons: nothing gives me joy when he is absent who alone gives joy.[32]

So far as it is possible to place side by side the analytical scheme of the nights and the descriptive account of the espousals and spiritual marriage, the deepest period of the night of the spirit, which is the divine light experienced as darkness, the divine immensity and excellence pressing upon the creature's narrow capacity and nothingness, would seem to take place after the espousals:

Our Lord Jesus . . . allows the soul to be tested by spiritual trials till the rust of impurity is burnt out of it. Interiorly such fears and doubts and perplexities will arise that the soul will almost fall into despair. It will seem to be forsaken by God and delivered into the hands of the devil, except that it will always have a little secret trust in the goodness and mercy of God. . . . It will be tried exteriorly as well, and suffer much pain in its bodily senses either through illness or through physical suffering caused by the devil. Or again by the secret operation of God the soul will suffer so mysteriously through its union with this wretched body that it would not be able to remain united to the body, if Our Lord Jesus did not enable it. . . . "My child, if you pass through fire, do not fear, for the flame shall not hurt you" (Is. 43. 2). It will cleanse you from all

[32] *Sermons on the Canticle*, Sermon 74, in *S. Bernardi Opera* edited by J. Leclercq (Rome, 1958), II, 242–4.

defilement of the flesh and make you able to receive the spiritual fire of the love of God.[33]

What follows is put by Hilton in sober words:

The more stable grace is, the less interrupted, the more beautiful is the soul and the more like to Him in whom, as the Apostle says, there is no change. And it is fitting that the soul should be like its divine spouse in behaviour and in virtue, fully resembling Him in the stability of perfect love. But that occurs rarely, and only in the chosen spouses of Christ.... For the purpose of all the divine action in a soul is to unite it to Him in the most perfect love.... To a pure soul whose eyes have been opened to the perfection of love, spiritual truths are revealed, not that the soul should rest in them, and seek no further, but that through them it should be led to seek and love Him who is above all, paying no attention to anything outside Him.[34]

And St John of the Cross:

In this state the soul sees that God truly belongs to it, and that it possesses Him with hereditary possession, with rightful ownership, as an adopted child of God, through the grace that God gave to it, and it sees that, since He belongs to it, it may give and communicate Him to whomsoever it desires of its own will; and thus it gives Him to its Beloved, Who is the very God that gave Himself to it. And herein the soul pays God all that it owes Him; inasmuch as, of its own will, it gives as much as it has received of Him.[35]

Recent historians of spirituality have taken to classing mystics according to their emphasis on union (*Brautmsytik*) or the transcendent Deity (*Wesensmystik*). The division is perhaps unreal, for love and knowledge enter into any approach to God, and into the most sublime infusion of contemplation, and whereas in love there can be union, in knowledge, while

[33] *Scale of Perfection*, II xxviii 223–5.
[34] *Ibid.*, II xli 283.
[35] *Living Flame*, second redaction, III par. 78 (Peers, III 184).

the soul is still in this life, God must always be seen in deeper ignorance and darkness.

A commentary on this can be found in the Italian medieval mystic, Blessed Angela of Foligno:

> I saw God in darkness, and necessarily in darkness, for He is too far above the mind for aught else, and everything that can be the object of thought has no proportion to Him. It was an unspeakable delight in the good that contains all that is, and nothing there can be the object of a word or an idea. I see nothing, I see all .... The power, the wisdom, the will of God, which I have seen wonderfully at other times, seem less than this. This is all; the others are as it were parts. In the boundless darkness, I see the Holy Trinity.[36]

In the higher stages of the mystical life the simple infusion of obscure knowledge and love is not the only form that "contemplation" takes. As the divine action becomes more frequent and more powerful, the soul begins to know by experience the different levels of its perceptive and receptive action. In the prayer of quiet, as very many mystics have described it, the soul can remain in supernatural recollection while the imagination is intensely active. At a later stage, the soul can perceive its own perception and life as distinct from, and far more capacious and multiform than, that of the reasoning mind, and the person can remain calm and untouched in soul while body and mind are under attack or in distress. Such a soul can also "see" the souls around it as clearly as the eye can see the body and as the mind can appreciate intellectual qualities and moral characteristics. An ability of this kind also extends to the perception of the presence of pure spirit. Excessive as was the importance attached in the medieval world and in too many later Catholic moral theologians to the part played by evil spirits in human affairs, and crude, grotesque and disgusting as was often the folklore of piety in ages when witches were harried and burnt

---

[36] *Book of visions and instructions*, ch. 26.

all over Europe, the existence of spiritual evil personified is
a fact of evangelical teaching and Christian experience, and
the mystic can be aware of the contact of good and evil as a
fearful presence of confusion, despair and the void of God and
all good things.

In the realm of contemplative knowledge, the darkness of
the transcendent Being is replaced at times by the brightest
flash of spiritual lightning which shows the truths of the faith
with a momentary clarity which often leaves its effects upon
the soul for many days, or it may be for a lifetime. An abiding
sense of the Three Persons of the Holy Trinity in the soul,
a realization of the truth held in blind faith by all Christians,
is found in almost all the mystics. It is apparent in its fullest
and clearest expression in the *Living Flame* and *Spiritual
Canticle* of St John of the Cross. It is recurrent in the life of
several modern mystics, particularly in that of Sister Elizabeth
"of the Trinity", from her early realization of "being dwelt in"
by God to her later constant references to "my Three" as
present in her soul.[37] Another experience of mature mystical
life is that called by St John "the intuition of naked truths":

> This kind of knowledge is of God Himself, and the delight
> is in God Himself, whereof David says: "There is naught
> soever like to Him." For this kind of knowledge comes to the
> soul in direct relation to God, when the soul, after a most
> lofty manner, has a perception of some attribute of God—of
> His omnipotence, of His might, of His goodness and sweetness.
> ... Inasmuch as this is pure contemplation, the soul clearly
> sees that there is no way wherein it can say aught concerning
> it, save to speak, in certain general terms, of the abundance
> of delight and blessing which it has felt, and this is expressed
> by souls that experience it; but not to the end that what the
> soul has experienced and perceived may be wholly appre-
> hended.[38]

[37] *Spiritual Doctrine of Sister Elizabeth of the Trinity*, ch. III.
[38] *Ascent of Mount Carmel*, II xxvi (Peers, I 182–3).

There are two other mystical experiences which, though not precisely contemplation, if this be defined as an inflowing of simple and obscure divine knowledge, are yet closely connected with it. There is, first, that called the experience of substantial interior words which are, as it were, the echo in the soul of the action upon it of the divine power:

> It is as if Our Lord were to say formally to the soul . . . "Love thou Me"; it would then have and feel within itself the substance of love for God. Or as if it feared greatly and He said to it: "Fear thou not"; it would at once feel within itself great fortitude and tranquillity. For the saying of God, and His Word, as the Wise Man says, is full of power; and thus that which He says to the soul He produces substantially within it. For it is this that David meant when he said: "See, He will give to His voice a voice of virtue". . . . With respect to these words, the soul should do nothing. It should neither desire them nor refrain from desiring them; it should neither reject them nor fear them. It should do nothing in the way of executing what these words express, for these substantial words are never pronounced by God in order that the soul may translate them into action, but that He may so translate them within the soul.[39]

Hence, unlike locutions of other kinds and visions they can be, and indeed must be, received in tranquillity:

> For this cause God says through Jeremias: "What has the chaff to do with the wheat? Are not My words surely as fire, and as a hammer that breaketh the rock to pieces?" And thus these words are greatly conducive to the union of the soul with God. . . . Happy is the soul to whom God addresses these words. Speak, Lord, for Thy servant heareth.[40]

The second is what are called "substantial touches":

> This is normally a most sublime perception of God . . . to which no name can be given, any more than to the feeling

[39] *Ibid.*, II xxxi (Peers, I 205).
[40] *Ibid.*, II xxxi (Peers, I 207).

whence it overflows.... The feelings which we have described
are produced passively in the soul, without any effective assistance on its own part; even so, likewise, is the knowledge of
them received passively in the understanding, in a way called
by the philosophers "passible", wherein the understanding plays
no part.... Let the soul be resigned, humble and passive herein,
for, since it receives this knowledge passively from God, He
will communicate it whensoever He is pleased, if He sees the
soul to be humble and detached. And in this way the soul will
do nothing to counteract the help which these kinds of knowledge give it in its progress towards divine union, which help
is great; for these touches are all touches of union, which is
wrought passively in the soul.[41]

It has sometimes been held, particularly by those who have
regarded the mystical experience as lying outside the normal
Christian economy of grace, that an imperfect or even a sinful
soul may be raised to contemplation by God; that, in other
words, contemplation neither presupposes nor implies the
previous possession of a markedly high degree of sanctifying
grace and divine charity. In this matter absolute clarity of
terms is necessary. We must first distinguish "contemplation"
from visions or what are called locutions (words heard from
an unseen source). These latter, once granted their possibility,
may come to imperfect and even sinful souls for whatever
their nature they affect the faculties, not the soul itself. Scripture has numerous instances. We must also allow for the possibility of a particularly powerful "operant" grace which bestows
at one and the same moment the first sanctifying grace and the
capacity to receive grace in some higher form. The penitent
thief of Calvary and Saul on the road to Damascus may be
instances of such sudden uncovenanted outpourings of grace.
But if by contemplation we mean infused knowledge and
love of the degree associated with union or even with the
fully developed prayer of quiet, and if by sinful we mean, not

[41] *Ibid.*, II xxxii (Peers, I 208-9).

necessarily gravely evil, but at least persistence in a state of carelessness and bad habits, in which the supposed "contemplation" is an isolated incident, then the answer must be firmly negative. If by definition contemplation is the reception of infused light and love, then the recipient must be in a fit state of reception and must therefore emerge from the experience with a higher degree of sanctifying grace.

Assertions to the contrary will generally be found to rest ultimately on some statements of St Teresa, and these may be briefly examined. They will not in fact bear the weight of argument put upon them. St Teresa, as is generally admitted, often wrote impulsively; she is sometimes self-contradictory and in her earlier writings she lacks the firmness of terminology which she shows in her latest work. Moreover, her statements that contemplation may be given to a sinful person is clearly autobiographical, and reflects the saint's avoidance of any appearance of self-commendation. The crucial passages occur in *The Way of Perfection*:

> I will tell you, then, that God is sometimes pleased to show great favour to persons who are in an evil state [and to raise them to perfect contemplation], so that by this means He may snatch them out of the hands of the devil. It must be understood, I think, that such persons will not be in mortal sin at the time. They may be in an evil state, and yet the Lord will allow them to see a vision, even a very good one, in order to draw them back to Himself. But I cannot believe that He would grant them contemplation. For that is a divine union, in which the Lord takes His delight in the soul and the soul takes its delight in Him; and there is no way in which the Purity of the Heavens can take pleasure in a soul that is unclean.[42]

This passage, here printed in its fullest form, has a complicated history and appears in some editions in an abbreviated shape. In the above form, it appears in the earliest manuscript of the work, save for the words "and raise them to perfect

[42] *Way of Perfection*, xvi (Peers, II 65).

contemplation". In a later manuscript, in which St Teresa cancelled many of her more personal and colloquial passages, all after the word "devil" is omitted. When in this truncated state the words "and raise them to perfect contemplation" were added in a hand which is not that of St Teresa by a reader who lacked the guidance given by the cancelled passage and felt that the phrase "great favour" needed to be made more specific. If this is omitted, as not authentic, St Teresa, who is clearly referring to herself, is seen to affirm what is undoubtedly the general (and correct) teaching, namely, that a sinner, as such, cannot be raised to contemplation, even as a means of inspiring better thoughts. The context makes it clear that St Teresa is not considering such extraordinary cases as that of St Paul.

Much use has also been made of another passage from St Teresa which runs as follows:

> I know there are many people who practise vocal prayer in the manner already described [i.e., the meditative use of the petitions of the Our Father] and are raised by God to the higher kind of contemplation without knowing how it has happened. I know a nun who could never practise anything but vocal prayer but who kept to this and found she had everything else.... She came to me once in great distress, saying that she did not know how to practise mental prayer, and that she could not contemplate but could only say vocal prayers. I asked her what prayers she said and I saw that, though keeping to the Paternoster, she was experiencing pure contemplation, and the Lord was raising her to be with Him in union. She spent her life so well, too, that her actions made it clear she was receiving great favours. So I praised the Lord and envied her vocal prayer.[43]

This passage has been used to support the opinion that vocal prayer, liturgical or private, is as fully adequate as mental prayer for a soul striving to advance in the love of

[43] *Ibid.*, xxx (Peers, II 126).

God, and that the grace of contemplative prayer may be granted to a soul who has never practised the latter. Nothing could be further from the saint's intention. It is clear from her words that the nun, known in other respects as a fervent religious, was in fact capable of a deep recollection while engaged in the recitation of the words of the Paternoster (the Divine Office does not enter into the narrative) and so was in fact far advanced in "mental prayer". Deep recollection in God, whenever and however attained or bestowed, is the end of all prayer, and to recall a soul from that in order to practise "mental prayer" would be more absurd than the practice, said to be met with in hospitals, of waking a patient from deep sleep in order that he may take the prescribed soporific drug. Formal "mental prayer" is not a spiritual panacea, the sesame that opens every door. Love alone, however manifested, leads to union with God. A person can meditate, recite the Office, assist at or even offer Mass without direct and conscious advertence and love. He can also, as all know well, spend a time allotted to mental prayer without advertence and love. Contrariwise, all lawful or prescribed actions can be turned into acts of the love of God. But of all regular means (excluding sacramental grace) for increasing the love and recollection of the soul "mental" prayer is the most potent, for it attains of itself directly to the definition of prayer, the rising of the mind to God.

CHAPTER XI

CONTEMPLATION AND NEOPLATONISM

The history, and perhaps also the practice, of Christian spirituality has been influenced by Neoplatonism so vitally that some account must be given of the process even in the shortest survey.

Neoplatonism is the modern name given to the doctrines of thinkers from the third century A.D. onwards who regarded themselves as Platonists, faithfully reproducing and extending the thought of their great master who had taught at Athens in the fourth century before Christ. In fact, and especially in the person and teaching of their earliest and greatest master Plotinus, the doctrines of Plato (and to a lesser extent those of Aristotle) were used as the basis of an original system of thought which was more complete and consistent than that of Plato. In this system a universe of spirit and thought, the emanation from a super-essential Being, was in perpetual outward and reflex movement. In it, the individual spirit aimed at purification and union with the One, in effect an impersonal Deity, by means of contemplation and ecstatic love. Plotinus was prejudiced against Christianity as he saw it, and was probably uninfluenced by its doctrines, but his ethical austerity, his high idealism and his near-Christian conception of the Godhead were all calculated to appeal to Christian thinkers in search of a system, and the adoption of much of the teaching of Plotinus by Augustine, the greatest and most permanently influential of the western Fathers, had an incalculable influence on western spirituality and mystical thought and sentiment. This was increased again by the Syrian monk at the beginning of the sixth century who published his writings under the name of Denis the Areopagite. Deeply impregnated with Neoplatonic terms and ideas, Denis was accepted as the Athenian convert of St Paul and in consequence enjoyed a semi-apostolic authority. His short practical treatise on mystical theology became a textbook that was cited and commented upon throughout the Middle Ages, and it was not till the fifteenth century that the Dionysian authorship was challenged. As a result of this transmission of ideas, the spiritual writings of the masters of the contemplative life in the Middle Ages in western Europe were saturated with expressions and doctrines which derived, at first or second hand, from Neoplatonic sources, and an amalgam of traditional Christian and Neo-platonizing Christian teaching was formed. On four points in particular doctrines, originally Neoplatonic, were firmly embedded in western Catholic thought. One was that the ascent of the soul to God was achieved by a series of negative resolutions by which all sight and sound at every level of the external world was progressively blotted out of the mind. Another was that the mystical illumination of the mind was sudden and brief, and that the end of the process was ecstasy. A third, a corollary of the first, was that the divine light was always ready to flood into the mind when the obstacles of sense and intellectual perception were removed. A fourth, consequent upon the first and third, was the assertion or rather the assumption that the progress of the soul to God was open to all who were capable of following the instructions as to moral and intellectual purity, and that therefore the goal of mystic illumination was open to all endowed with the requisite gifts and the strength to persevere. As a consequence of this "contamination" it became (and still remains) very difficult

when examining spiritual writers of all centuries to dissever
the traditional Christian teaching and the experiential wisdom
of the Church from the doctrines, which may or may not be
viable in a Christian context, of a wholly non-Christian system
of thought. While the gain to mystical theology from the ideas
and methods of the most spiritual and theistic of all ancient
thinkers is undoubted, the accretion to Catholic spiritual theology of purely speculative propositions and techniques has
brought with it confusions and problems not a few.

The marriage between theology and philosophy, and even
the service to theology of philosophy in its traditional ancil-
lary position, has always been an uneasy one, liable to mis-
haps. The conviction upon which all attempts at a peaceful
symbiosis rests, that all human minds functioning rightly must
necessarily agree on a single catalogue of answers to the problems of the universe and of man's conduct therein, is subject
to such shocks of experience, and depends upon so many
conditions which cannot be realized in practice, that while it
may remain radically true as a proposition and a desire among
men of goodwill, it can be realized only among certain groups
and at certain moments of history. The conviction of St Augustine that Platonism (which was in fact Neoplatonism in his
day) was in essence the true answer of man's reason to the
riddle of the universe, added to the conviction of all western
writers some centuries later that the neoplatonizing pseudo-
Denis was a contemporary and close disciple of St Paul, had
as their result a strong contamination of Christian philosophical thought by Neoplatonic theories, and as Augustine and
Denis were the two pillars of early medieval mystical theory
the tendencies mentioned above permeated Christian spiritual
literature, were copied from book to book, were adopted in
different degrees by the scholastic theologians and have been
repeated down the centuries to our own time by those who
have not had the training or the facilities or the energy to
criticize what they have received from others. Additional con-

fusion on a considerable scale has also been caused by misconceived concordism, the natural desire to harmonize two
accepted authorities or to show that a desirable opinion is
expressed by a venerated master. Thus—to take two contrast-
ing examples of *bona fide* unconscious confusion—Dominican
writers have been at great pains to see in all instances of
St Thomas's use of the word "contemplation" an agreement
with the use of the word by the Spanish Carmelite mystics;
recent Jesuit writers have shown an equal desire to equate
St Ignatius's use of the word with the same Carmelite tradition. This is not to say that both parties have entirely falsified
the teaching of their masters. But it is certain, not as a matter
of speculation but as one of history and linguistics, that the
three schools in fact at times attach different meanings to a
single term, and that the different meanings reflect different
historical currents of thought.

The contamination of Christian mystical theology by Neoplatonism deserves a closer study than it has hitherto received.
Many non-Catholic writers have roundly asserted that the
whole body of Christian teaching on contemplation is a prolongation of Neoplatonic doctrine. Catholic writers, on the
other hand, have often either ignored Neoplatonic influence
or failed to isolate its character and extent. Thus the well-
known book of Abbot Cuthbert Butler, *Western Mysticism*,
though in the main a scholarly, original and important work
which still retains its authority, has a very misleading title
which the author defends in his book. Not only does he suggest
that there are a number of "mysticisms" in the Christian
Church, one of which is characteristic of the western patristic
period and is by implication more in harmony with western
European religious sentiment than is the eastern, Dionysian,
treatment, but he fails to realize that many of the characteristic
features of Augustine's and Gregory's teaching on contemplation derive from a Plotinian or Neoplatonic source and are
therefore alien to the pure Christian tradition which has con-

tinued to exist throughout the history of the Church, though overlaid from time to time by elements introduced from without. Thus the teaching that contemplation is a mental effort which is rewarded by a sudden dazzling flash of vision, followed by a sinking back of the exhausted spirit, as also the teaching that contemplation is the goal of the Christian's endeavour, are Christianized versions of Plotinian and Hellenic teaching which, earlier in St Gregory's century, was appearing in another and more logical presentation in the works of the pseudo-Denis.

A second wave of Neoplatonism washed into the schools of western Europe at the end of the twelfth century, when the Dionysian writings were translated and broadcast in the West in something like entirety for the first time. St Bonaventure's *Journey of the mind to God* is a wholly Christianized version of the Dionysian progress of the soul to ecstasy as mediated by St Augustine. The saint, it may be said summarily, substitutes love (charity) for knowledge (gnosis), but nevertheless the conception of an orderly advance ending in ecstatic union is Dionysian or Plotinian, not Christian. St Albert the Great was a closer disciple of the Areopagite, and the greatest of the Rhineland scholars, Master Eckhardt, built his original system wholly on Neoplatonic lines, though the framework is Aristotelian and Thomist. Eckhardt is wholly Neoplatonic in his conception of the whole Christian life as a growth in mystical enlightenment, but his disciple, John Tauler, eliminated much of the speculative element from his teaching and emphasized the traditional and practical part. What remained was the conception of the interior life as a progress of enlightenment in which the divine light poured into the soul in proportion to its success in stripping itself of all creatures and entering into darkness. Tauler comes very near to the application found later in Spanish theologians of the old maxim that nature abhors a vacuum, and that therefore divine light replaces immediately and inevitably the natural lights banished by a rigid process of exclusion. Later Dominican and other writers cut out almost all traces of Dionysian influence, but theologians of the school tended to take back this or that Dionysian thesis, particularly that of nature's abhorrence of a vacuum.

CHAPTER XII

QUIETISM

No sketch of Catholic mysticism would be complete without some mention of Quietism. Quietism, in the virulent form in which it was finally condemned, was almost entirely the teaching of a single not very distinguished man, the Spanish priest Michael de Molinos (1628–1717), a somewhat sinister figure whose misfortunes were familiar to English readers eighty years ago from the pages of the successful historical novel *John Inglesant*. The fulmination of the papal condemnation of Molinism was in many ways more destructive in its echo than in its blast, for it resulted in a misunderstanding and prejudice which lasted for almost a century and it has ever since been a bogey to scare the ill-informed.

Quietism took its rise at the tail of the spiritual movement, called by Henri Bremond *l'invasion mystique*, which broadcast the ascetical and mystical doctrines of the Spanish writers of the sixteenth century and made mental prayer and discussions on the spiritual life fashionable not only in Carmel and among the Visitandines of France but in devout and aristocratic circles in France, Italy, and the Netherlands, then partly under Spanish dominion. Mystic doctrine, which of its nature should be reserved for the few who are called to practise it, or who are at least vowed to a life of solitude and recollection, was a popular topic of discussion in polite circles, and in conferences as well as in confessionals, and it is not surprising that the true way of the contemplative was falsified, perverted and misunderstood. Molinos himself may have begun his career as a fashionable spiritual director in good faith, but his later conduct was at least equivocal. He taught all who came to him that the ideal of the mystical life was to attain complete silence and inaction in the interior powers, and to wait for the divine influence to come upon the soul. Later, he spread the more dangerous teaching that the would-be contemplative should establish himself in a state of passivity, making no attempt to repel evil thoughts or desires. When such a resolve of passivity had been taken, no action could be imputed as evil, however apparently sinful. Molinos himself was accused of using this teaching to seduce his penitents, and spent his latter years in the prisons of the Inquisition. A long series of propositions was extracted from his teaching and condemned, thirty years later, in the France of Bossuet and Fénelon, when Jansenism was beginning to act as a creeping paralysis of fervour. Fénelon, archbishop of Cambrai, was misled into defending his penitent Mme Guyon, who was at the time certainly practising a quietist form of piety, though without the dangerous moral undertones of Molinos. Semi-quietism, as it was called, was the ultimate result of the attempt to define and to attain "pure love"; Fénelon defended the opinion that contemplation resulted in a kind of annihilation of all personal interest or thought for one's salvation, and that this could become a permanent state of the contemplative soul. Fénelon's writings were condemned after a long and somewhat disedifying campaign conducted by Bossuet, but the manoeuvres of Fénelon himself were at times devious.

This controversy, on account of the eminence of the two champions, and the contrast of their characters and methods, has attracted the attention of many historians of literature and spirituality, and the sympathies of most of these have gone to the gentle and sympathetic archbishop of Cambrai rather than to the seemingly overbearing and rigid "eagle of Meaux". There can, however, be no question as to Bossuet's keenness of sight, now that all personal issues have dropped away, and the theological principles can be seen and checked against the traditional teaching of the mystics of earlier and later centuries.

The radical error of Quietism is unmistakable. It was based on a total misconception of grace and the supernatural life of the soul. It implied an almost mechanical conception of the spiritual life, and a denial of the freedom of God's grace. It was, in effect, an attempt to take the kingdom of God by violence—not as in our Lord's sense, by the impetuosity of faith and love, but by the sheer silencing of every movement of mind and will. If the natural powers were silenced, as it were by force, and complete quiescence were attained, God would then, sooner rather than later, raise the soul to contemplation, which was the only true form of Christian spirituality. This was a parody, complete but at first sight deceptive, of the traditional teaching recently broadcast by the followers of the Spanish mystics. These latter had taught that the soul must always give love to God either by its natural powers assisted by grace, or by the same powers moved freely but compulsively by God. The latter state, that of contemplatives, was not common, and could be prepared for only by sincere, and even severe, ascetical practice. In the transition between the human way of action and the mystical reception of the divine influence the faith and love of the soul might be at times almost imperceptible, but they were there; if not, the soul would be doing nothing, and would thus be unpleasing to God. Almost all the trouble was caused by the preaching to all and sundry of a kind of prayer proper only to a few, which Molinos (and perhaps others also) had fundamentally misunderstood and misrepresented. Unfortunately the condemnation of Quietism went into great detail and used ambiguous terms of mystical theology without giving clear definitions. It demanded at the time a delicate spiritual perception to see precisely what was condemned and what not,

and there were not wanting heresy-hunters who spread sus-
picion and misunderstanding. The net result was a flight from
mystical theology for more than a century, and a return to
the examination of external phenomena, such as visions, as
the best criterion of sanctity.

Semi-quietism contained error still more subtle and fair-
seeming, and some of the propositions condemned have such
an edifying ring as to cause a shock of surprise at first reading.
Weighed carefully, however, they will be seen to contain, in
weaker solution, the same rigidity, lack of humility, and
failure to bow to the necessity of grace. In their assertion of
the primacy, and indeed necessity, of pure love they fail to
distinguish between purely human love and the work of the
Holy Spirit in the soul, and between the human act assisted
by grace, and the infused love of the mystic. Thus the first
condemned proposition runs: "There exists an habitual state
of the love of God which is pure love without any admixture
of the motive of personal interest. Neither fear of punishment,
nor desire of reward, has any longer part therein. God is no
longer loved because of the merit of doing so, nor because
of the perfection of such love, nor because of the happiness
to be found in it."

Here the error lies partly in the word "habitual", and partly
in the rigid exclusion of all motive. Infused love, in the form
of operant grace, can be of perfect purity, but it is an act, not
a habit. Filial love, and still more the love of a soul in the
unitive way, drives out servile fear and self-regarding love,
but not the awe of God and the proper regard of self which
are essential to creaturely being and self-direction.

Another proposition runs: "One must annihilate one's
powers; this is the spiritual life. To want to work actively is
to offend God, who wishes himself to be the sole agent: and
thus one must lose oneself in God wholly and absolutely and
thenceforward remain as a dead body."

In the first sentence of this the principal error is in the word "annihilate". The mystic's powers are not annihilated, but so fully controlled and centred upon God that he can move them without any resistance or defection. In the second sentence there are two errors. First, our powers are given to be exercised; the function of grace, and the "wish of God" is that they should be directed to the fulfilling of his will by our own co-operation with grace. When this becomes complete, in the extreme case of the perfect soul, the human action may be called "divinized", but God is not the sole agent; the human will is intensely active but entirely united with or absorbed in that of God. The second error is another aspect of the first. The aim of the spiritual life is indeed to unite the soul to God, and the expression "abandon oneself" is tolerable, particularly in the Romance languages, but the goal must not be conceived as remaining as a dead body, but as one full of true life. The "dead body" was doubtless a reminiscence of a celebrated expression of St Ignatius (who himself was following St Francis) to describe religious obedience, but whatever may be thought of that metaphor it does not imply Quietism. The obedient religious may give his external activities, and even the employment of his mind, to the service of his superior, but he continues to operate actively; the corpse is entirely metaphorical; a literally dead body is of no use to God or man.

Quietism in its extreme form was a passing aberration not likely to return, and the controversy over pure love, though it may still tease the mind like a problem in logic, has ceased to agitate the theologians and does not exist for the true mystic. It is possible nevertheless for innocent quietists to exist today or in any age, either from a misunderstanding of the true and necessary teaching on the centring of the mind and will upon God alone, and the avoidance of all alien thoughts, or from a mistaken or uncritical exhortation or direction towards the prayer of simplicity when the soul so counselled is not in fact prepared and enabled by grace to abandon meditative or affective mental prayer. It is here, as has been suggested elsewhere, that serious harm may be done by indiscriminate recommendation of the prayer of simple recollection, and still more by the suggestion that it is the beginning of mystical prayer. It is the fault of some modern writers that they neglect the ascetic aspect of the spiritual life and fail to demand that generosity of soul which is a necessary condition of real spiritual progress. They apply to those who are beginners in the true sense of the word instructions which the masters reserve for the truly progressive. From this, the least harm that can follow is endless aridity and self-examination; at the worst there may be grave self-deception or the abandonment of all attempt to persevere in the practice of mental prayer.

The traditional teaching of the Christian Church on grace, founded upon the words of our Lord, the pronouncements of St Paul, and the essence (but not the entirety) of the treatises of St Augustine, is a straight path between naturalism (or, in theological terms, Pelagianism) and Quietism, or false supernaturalism. On the one hand, no amount of merely human or solely self-regarding effort can achieve any step in the way of salvation or sanctification: "Without me you can do nothing". On the other hand, God by his power, gentle but strong, does not save us from doing anything ourselves but aids us precisely so that we may act with great, even heroic, strength: "I can do all in him who strengthens me". Quietism, in the last analysis, while claiming to be abandonment to God, is in fact a refusal of God's help.

CHAPTER XIII

CAN THE FULL MYSTICAL EXPERIENCE BE FOUND OUTSIDE THE CHRISTIAN CHURCH?

Of all the problems that arise in the course of a discussion of mysticism, this is perhaps the one of the greatest general interest as it is also the most baffling. While it may be possible to propose a theoretical solution, this must at best be imprecise and inconclusive, for reasons that will be mentioned shortly. On the other hand, only observation and experience on a very wide scale would be sufficient to provide evidence of an empirical, existential character, and the topic is too recent and too difficult in itself to have provided as yet sufficient data. All that can be done is to set down what seem to be the theological principles, and then to consider what observation and experience may suggest.

We may begin by defining our terms of reference. We shall shortly consider "natural" mysticism, the intuitional apprehension of unity, truth, beauty and love in the universe of being as it is presented to a human mind. Authentic as such apprehensions undoubtedly are, and genuine as is the religious character they may assume in the minds of those who believe in God or in the Christian revelation, they are not identical, or of the same species, as the infused knowledge and love of God himself which the mystics claim to have experienced. This distinction will naturally be denied by those to whom all mysticism is a purely psychological phenomenon, but this denial follows a division between believers and non-believers which cannot be avoided. We are speaking for the moment of the higher manifestations of knowledge and love supernaturally received.

As has repeatedly been stated, such manifestations are in the free gift of God, whose hand is not shortened and whose love keeps all his creatures in being. For their bestowal, there-fore, we can lay down no laws. Whether, or when, God bestows these gifts on those who have given no sign of their belief in his existence can be ascertained, if at all, only by evidence of occurrence. We can, however, say that for souls, Christian or pagan, to be recipients they must have a receptive power, the habit of what we call sanctifying grace, either pre-viously existing in the soul or infused prior (at least logically) to the mystical experience. There is, however, no theological difficulty in supposing that God may give such graces to non-Catholic baptized Christians or to those outside any visible Christian fold who believe in a personal, loving Creator and Sustainer. Whether or not mystical graces are ever or often given to believers of this kind must be a matter of evidence; there is no problem here save the universal problem of pre-destination. The real problem lies with the alleged philo-sophical mystics and with the great non-Christian world-religions.

Of the former class Plotinus is usually taken as the supreme example of those of whom we have anything like adequate documentation. As is well known, he is represented (for the *Enneads* are his teaching, not his own writing) as having ex-perienced on a few rare occasions, of which his biographer Porphyry vouches for four during the six years of their com-panionship, attained to (or received) a unitive ecstasy in which he was in an inexpressible way conscious of direct contact with the One above all categories of being. We are told by Porphyry that such experiences were extremely rare, and they do not form an essential key to his philosophical system, nor are there any similar well-authenticated ecstasies in the records of Neoplatonism. Nevertheless, these incidents in the life of Plotinus have been universally accepted as authentic accounts of actual experiences, and some Christian, as well as all non-Christian, writers have accepted them as being on an equality with the highest experiences of the Christian mystics.

It can be argued that this is to go beyond the evidence. That evidence shows these experiences to be infrequent and the result of a methodical effort of abstraction. No claim is made that the philosopher saw a richness or a depth of being in the Deity, but merely that he was conscious of some kind of union with the absolute One, a union which was a union of love and perfect happiness. Is this identical with the continual, quasi-habitual union of the Christian mystics, with its range of vision (apprehended but not communicable) over the inner life of the Trinity and over the divine guidance of the universe? Some have hesitated to pronounce, while implicitly accepting the identity. Others have allowed that a soul of exceptional purity and intellectual power received grace from the Father of Light. Others again may think that this was the extreme limit of the capacity of the Greek genius, seen earlier in similar, though not identical, experiences of Plato and Socrates, to rise above sense-perceptions and the dialectical process to a momentary apprehension or intuition of the God of what is called natural religion, the One absolute Being in whom all other intelligences have their being and their existence. To the present writer the last answer appears to be the true one. The great difference between the Plotinian and the Christian unions is not so much in the preponderantly intellectual nature of the former as in its "active", that is its self-centred, character. It is an attainment, a result of effort, of abstraction, and the reward is a sight of truth and beauty, and a bliss which comes from the mind's adequate sight of its object and of its reality. There is none of that awareness of the nothing of all being as against the true Being of God, and of the new, God-given capacity of loving without any trace of self-love both God and all his creatures to the degree that they bear his likeness. It lacks the humility, the receptiveness and the sense of meeting between spirit and Spirit. It seems to demand an intellectual power and a natural strength of will and mind capable of attaining by an intense effort of mental abstraction to a victory, as one might say, over all the un-intellectual components of the human personality, a victory as brief as it is marvellous. The Christian mystic needs no great intellectual power. God has chosen the weak things of the world to confound those who are strong. The forgetfulness of self, which is the condition without which nothing can be done, is made possible by the poverty of spirit which itself is a divine gift. The Carmelite lay-sister, not to say the Virgin of Nazareth, can have a union with God far more sublime than that of the Greek philosopher. To say this is not to diminish the authenticity and even the sublimity of the Plotinian ecstasy, but to mark off the wholly supernatural from what is a lesser gift of God. This judgement will be incomprehensible to one who does not take cognizance of any capacity higher than what is human, but the lack of agreement is the same with regard to the gift of Christian faith.

As regards the world-religions, and in particular Muslims and Buddhists, only those with a competent knowledge both of Christian theology and with the beliefs and history of these religious bodies have any right to give an opinion. The followers of the Prophet believe in one God, whom they expressly identify with the God of the Jews and Christians. Among the Buddhists also there seem to be clear indications of belief in a single all-powerful God, at least in some of the monastic bodies. Among both Buddhists and Muslims there is a large body of what may fairly be called mystical experience and writing. Whether this is in the strictly theological sense supernatural mysticism, that is, an incommunicable knowledge of God above anything that the unaided mind and soul can attain, or whether it is the knowledge of the Deity attained by a pure soul and mind assisted by divine grace but not enriched by infused knowledge and love only one equipped both spiritually and theologically would be fit to judge. One point is clear. If God, who is the common Father of all men, allows himself to be known by those outside the body of the faithful of his Church—and Christ himself praised the centurion for a faith that he had not found in Israel—the God so attained is the very God who sent his Son to redeem mankind, whose name is the only Name in whom mankind may be saved. Whether it is his will so to manifest himself to those outside his Church we cannot say. But we can at least say that more than a mere verbal resemblance is needed to establish identity of experience between Christian and non-Christian. The mystical experience, whether supernatural or what is called philosophical or nature mysticism, is by definition inexpressible. By their fruits you shall know them. Ardent love, self-sacrifice, wisdom and clarity of vision are the signs of true Christian mysticism—above all, perhaps, the abiding realization of union with a transcendent, infinite Being beyond all knowledge. It is not attained by mental concentration or by intellectual abstraction or by effort of the will, but by outgoing love which is taken up and transferred into the love of God in God.

CHAPTER XIV

NATURE MYSTICISM

What is the relationship of Christian, "supernatural", mysticism to what is called "nature mysticism"? The very form of words answers, or as some would say begs, the whole question. For those who hold that the one results from the action of God on the soul, while the other is a normal, if unfamiliar, activity of the mind no further answer is required. It may, however, be of use to put the question in other words, and to ask, "what *is* nature—or natural mysticism?"

Nature mysticism as an explicit and declared form of mental experience is of relatively modern appearance. It differs from Platonic, philosophical, idealist mysticism, which has reappeared from time to time in the modern world, in the absence from it of all reasoning or speculation. It is an intuition, which is sometimes so vivid as to appear to be a vision, of reality and unity in the world "outside" the mind. In its most precisely definable form it is associated with natural beauty and sublimity or with a quasi-personified "nature" as its object. The fact that the poets Wordsworth and Tennyson and the writer Richard Jefferies have been cited times out of mind seems to show that the expression of this experience is a modern one and not common. Its classic expression has usually been found in Wordsworth's *Lines composed above Tintern Abbey*, in his *Ode to the Intimations of Immortality*, and to some passages written in his early manhood which were later embodied in *The Prelude*. It is perhaps one kind, one manifestation, so to say, of the poetic experience itself, but unlike other manifestations—the poetic expression of passionate love, for example, or of the recognition of human mortality and natural mutability—it seems to give an insight into the very nature and constitution of the universe, and to reveal an identity, or at least a very real relationship, between the individual and the whole, together with an enhancement of delight and a sense that if one could see a shade deeper all contradictions and bitterness of division might be resolved. These may seem exaggerated expressions to some, as some also are deaf to music or without any experience of "romantic" love, but many will recognize them as true. They may even remember, and that throughout a long life, a few such moments of vision which have never wholly lost their spell, their sesame, that reopens a casement upon magic seas. These moments are not always associated with natural beauty. The pattern and conduct of life, or the disposition of the providence of God, may be their basis. Those who have experienced them will in general agree with Wordsworth that they are most frequent in the years of adolescence between, say, twelve and the mid-twenties, after which they "fade into the light of common day". This would be a further indication, if one were needed, that they are the result of experience upon a psychological organism at an early stage of its maturity; after that, "feeling" gives way to "reflection", or to the sadness of Keats's "the feel of not-to-feel it". Yet if they no longer recur they may remain as landmarks of the past that still remain to guide the present. Wordsworth, in many a passage, has given eloquent and moving utterance to this conviction:

> I at this time, [he was rising seventeen]
> Saw blessings spread around me like a sea,
> From Nature and her overflowing soul
> I had received so much, that all my thoughts
> Were steeped in feeling; I was only then
> Contented, when with bliss ineffable

I felt the sentiment of Being spread
O'er all that moves and all that seemeth still;
O'er all that, lost beyond the reach of thought
And human knowledge, to the human eye
Invisible, yet liveth to the heart;
   .   .   .   Wonder not
If high the transport, great the joy I felt
Communing in this sort through earth and heaven
With every form of creature, as it looked
Towards the Uncreated with a countenance
Of adoration, with an eye of love.
One song they sang, and it was audible,
Most audible, then, when the fleshly ear
O'ercome by humblest prelude of that strain,
Forgot her functions, and slept undisturbed.[1]

It will be seen that in their combination of vivid experience,
incommunicable certainty and joy and lasting impression
they have an external resemblance, if no more, to supernatural mystical experiences as described by those familiar
with them, and those who either deny or misconceive the supernatural, or who attach so much importance to their intuitions
that they transfer them to a higher order than is right, will naturally stress this resemblance. Like mystical experiences, also,
their truth is in inverse proportion to their intelligibility; when
we try to analyse or to explain, they fade into thin air and elude
our grasp. Wordsworth's celebrated lines describe both the
intuition and its permanence:

Those shadowy recollections,
   Which, be they what they may,
Are yet a master-light of all our seeing;
   Uphold us, cherish, and have power to make
Our noisy years seem moments in the being
   Of the eternal Silence: truths that wake,
      To cherish never.[2]

[1] *The Prelude*, Book II, near end.
[2] *Ode to the Intimations of Immortality*.

In these lines, indeed, he sees these experiences in what is remarkably like the Platonic presentation of the present life as a phase in the existence of an immortal being, but this is not his ordinary attitude to them, nor is it one that has been recorded by the many who have had experiences of the kind. To few, perhaps, has the intuition been so vivid and its influence so great.

Akin to nature mysticism in substance, though not in the surrounding circumstances, are the "moments of vision", often of very great intensity and abiding influence, that have come to individuals of the most diverse characters and classes. Their authenticity as genuine and profound mental experiences is not in doubt. That they cannot be exactly described is no argument against their reality. The poetic, the musical or the aesthetic experience is as real, indeed more real, than the registration by the mind of physical pleasure or pain. They do, however, raise a problem as to their object and origin, which the others do not. Do they, so to say, raise a veil that normally covers a deeper kind of reality than that of daily experience? Have they an origin external to the mind of the individual to whom they come? The answer to the first question would seem to be that they stand to the everyday intuitional mental life as metaphysical reasoning stands to scientific observation. To the second question the simple answer would be: No. But those who either by reason, or still more by faith, maintain the existence of a provident God, or of a loving incarnate Redeemer—a God both transcendent and immanent—will not readily say what reflections of his light and love may not be present, for in him we live and move and have our being. While it is easy, and doubtless often true, to say that the religious colour which many of these moments of vision assume is due to the thoughts and beliefs already latent in the mind, the Spirit of Truth may also be working invisibly.

This possibility becomes more significant in the "conversion experiences" which are common to all the Christian Churches and even to those of no confessional allegiance. In some of them the change of life, and the mental, moral and spiritual development that follows are so clear that the problem of the quality of the experience does not exist for any who believe in God. We may reject the word "mystical" in connection with the conversion of St Paul or St Augustine without questioning the supernatural agency at work. The problem exists rather in those cases when the person concerned claims some kind of contact with God or with the Redeemer which gives an assurance of salvation or a conviction of God's love. The first-hand and clearly authentic examples among the Quakers and Methodists in the seventeenth and eighteenth centuries and later, and the oft-quoted night of Fire of Pascal, are instances. In almost all these cases, and specifically in that of Pascal, the experience is the term of a long and often bitter mental or moral strife, which may be thought to have had a great part in the *dénouement*. Pascal's celebrated experience, authentic as it undoubtedly was, was the moment of resolution for a mind of almost unique capacity in the toils of an agonizing crisis of faith. Who shall say what element of grace was present and was seen as a vision of fire? Certainly, if we must theorize about it, the cool but not unsympathetic analysis of Henri Bremond is more satisfying than the enthusiastic acceptance of Abbot Cuthbert Butler. Certainly to regard it as a mystical experience of a high order would run counter to the teaching of the greatest mystics, and indeed every detail and aspect of it has been a target for criticism.

CHAPTER XV

CONCLUSION

As a conclusion to this study it may be well to give a brief summary of the main lines of thought that have been followed.

Mysticism, always an ambiguous term since its modern birth, became a common topic for discussion and research among believers and unbelievers alike less than a century ago, largely as a result of the new approach to psychology in the schools of Europe and to the reaction in the Anglo-Saxon world in face of the rationalist and materialist attacks upon revealed religion. This study, developed principally by those unacquainted with and uninterested in theology, approached the subject from an empirical standpoint, even when treated by Catholic writers and thinkers, and the great Catholic mystics were regarded as a part only, if perhaps an extremely important part, of the apologetic support provided by mysticism as an essential element of religion and as an assertion of the spiritual as against the materialistic interpretation of the universe.

After a considerable time Catholic theologians and spiritual writers began to take cognizance of the new debate and the large field that was opening out, and when at length they intervened it soon became clear that the mystical life had from the very beginnings of Christianity formed a part, and the highest part, of the sanctified life of the soul, and that the evidence of the mystics, and the writings of the Fathers and theologians, had together built up a body of theoretical and

practical teaching which had been almost entirely ignored by
the purely empirical and existentialist approach of modern
thinkers. This theological exposition, which careful examination has shown to be both traditional in the fullest sense of
the word and also entirely in harmony with the personal
witness of Christian mystics from the time of St Paul to our
own day, should therefore form the basis of any Catholic
exposition of mysticism. Catholic Christian mystical theology,
sufficiently controlled by experience, should for Christians
be a basic authoritative discipline, which alone can give the
true explanation, so far as an explanation is possible, of the
mystical way of life. It would indeed be strange if Christian
theology, after two thousand years of religious experience,
were unable to account for the highest manifestations of the
life of grace. Once these principles have been established, the
Christian student and writer can then proceed to discuss
apparently similar teaching and experience outside the Church,
and to decide how far the appearances of mysticism are
identical in all or some or no respects. The Christian is committed to a firm belief that a divine Person, who is also a
human being, Christ Jesus, loves and aids and inspires every
human soul that knows him by faith and love; he cannot
accept any opinion which rests on the assumption that all
human knowledge and activity is independent of any higher
influence from the world of spirit, or that sees in the universe
that is revealed to our senses and examined by our mind the
sum total of existing being.

Seen thus as an integral part of the Christian traditional and
scriptural teaching, "mysticism" appears as the culmination of
the spiritual life of grace which is in essence the achievement
of a union of love between God and the human soul, reborn
in a higher, "supernatural", life by the grace of Christ the
Saviour. This union of love, which Scripture and the liturgy do
not hesitate to call a sharing in the divine nature, and which
traditional theology, as well as the mystics themselves, de-

scribe as a "deification", can only be attained by a mind and will endowed with God-given faith, trust and love. These are the endowment of every baptized Christian who has not grievously offended God, and they have as their foundation the Holy Spirit present and active in the soul. They can and should develop, along with all the other endowments of the soul, throughout life, which is itself the beginning of eternal life. At a certain spiritual level determined by the providence of God, the action of the Holy Spirit, from being an imperceptible aid and inspiration and light, becomes, at first rarely but later almost continuously, a source of a new knowledge and love of God, which in its fullest growth is an effluence of the love and knowledge which God has of himself and which enters into the relationships of the divine Persons. This knowledge is still to the soul obscure and this love is of itself too deep for feeling, but the knowledge and love are intimately and most vividly experienced in an inexpressible way by the soul and recognized also in their effects by the soul and others. This is the mystical life, which increases in depth and becomes the rarer of attainment the purer it is. As it grows, the union of the soul and the divine Word becomes more complete and the knowledge more perfect, not by the comprehension of the Divinity, which can only be achieved in the light of glory in the eternal life, but in an increasing clarity of perception both of what is not God and of what God is not, and an increasing apprehension, arising from the likeness that love bestows, of the truth and beauty of all that he has revealed of himself and his ways. Within this mystical life God may also by special illumination of the mind and touches of love in the will lift, as it were, a corner of the veil that hides his infinite perfection from all created understanding.

This life, though it is a prolongation of the life of grace that is shared by all Christians, and though it consists primarily in the fulfilment of the First Commandment of the Law and of Christ, differs from the common life of grace in kind, not only in degree. It is bestowed as freely and as independently of merit as is the gift of faith, whether in the grown man or the baptized infant. A virtuous life does not of itself lead on to mystical grace, yet the gift is normally not given to a soul unprepared. Sometimes it can be seen as the term or consummation of a long progress, but more often the soul that receives it has been exceptionally endowed and adorned with grace, and called from infancy or childhood.

The mystical life, which is the Christian life raised to a higher "power", shows therefore, though at a higher level of perfection, the two essentials of every Christian life, the union, or identification, with Christ, and the love of others in Christ and in God. Union with Christ, taken to its furthest perfection, is a union also with his redemptive love and sufferings in a way that lies beyond the experience and even beyond the imagination of most Christians. This love of others, which appears as an ardent and practical force in daily life, can also rise far above the normal experience to a level of self-dedication and to the satisfaction, by love and suffering, for the faults of others. In its perfect form of true substitution this can be achieved only in the mystic way when the soul in union with Christ is able in that union to offer itself to the Father in a sacrifice of praise and immolation.

The mystical life in its higher reaches is very rare, as are all supreme excellencies of any kind. In no sphere does God give equal gifts to all, nor on any level are all faithful to the same degree in their use of the talents they have received. At every stage a soul can refuse or fail. Many are called, but few are chosen. But whereas we must believe that a soul cannot be lost unless it has refused an invitation, a "sufficient" grace that could have led it to salvation, it is not clear that every soul in grace is called to the mystical life in the same way that it is called, and has it within its power, grace accompanying, to reach its allotted measure of virtuous excellence. The Spirit of God may lead it to the pastoral or missionary

life, or to a life of devoted service of others. But that all
Christians are called, at least remotely by the words of Christ
and the constant partaking of the Body and Blood of the
Saviour, to the perfect following of Christ is not doubtful, and
the perfect following of Christ demands, and surely receives,
a perceptible illumination and strengthening that is infused
and at least in part mystical. Christians sometimes encounter
in those outside their faith a charity and self-sacrifice that
amazes them and puts them to shame. The sentiment of
humility does them credit, but if they are tempted to ask:
what then does our faith do for us? they should look upon
the perfection to which they are called by the Gospel of Christ,
and to which the mystics of our day still attain, and they will
then measure their lowliness not only against their neighbour's
goodness, but against the infinite beauty of God.

The true mystic travels by love through darkness, a darkness which is in fact the rejection, for love's sake, of everything that is not God. Only those who are called and who go
by this way will come to the fullness of mystical union. There
are many mansions, and God has many ways of dealing with
souls. Many things that appear as marvels to some—visions,
locutions, raptures—are in fact often the by-product, so to say,
of spiritual graces which the soul is not strong enough to
receive as such. For some these perceptible husks of spiritual
grace may be necessary at an early stage of their spiritual lives;
the case of St Teresa is an eminent example, and there is
contemporary evidence for at least some such phenomena in
the early life of St John of the Cross, who so relentlessly,
apparently with the Mother Foundress in mind, made war
against those who put their trust in visions. For indeed, visions
and all other psycho-physical manifestations are neither mysticism nor a direct preparation for it.

The development of the mystical life in its early stages can
be seen most clearly in the way of prayer of the person concerned. That prayer has been taken as a kind of yardstick

universally since the sixteenth century, but scarcely ever in the ages previous to that, can be explained by the history of Christian spirituality in the Middle Ages. Prayer, it need scarcely be said, and prayer in both its public and private forms, had always been a vital part of a Christian life, but set "mental prayer" and "meditation" considered as a regulated and integral element in daily religious life appeared for the first time in the fifteenth century in two regions of Europe. In the Rhineland and Low Countries pietistic meditation on the life and passion of Christ became a regular feature of the devout life, while in Italy meditation as a set exercise of monastic life formed part of the reform of Santa Giustina at Padua and spread thence to Spain, where it formed part of the spiritual background to the teaching of Ignatius of Loyola and the Franciscan and Carmelite reforms. When "meditation" became universally recognized as the starting-point of all instruction in prayer, mental prayer, with its gradual growth in simplicity and its eventual change from active to infused love and knowledge, became the simplest thermometer of spiritual advance. But we must not forget that the Christian grows in similarity to Christ by love, not precisely by prayer, and in a recollected and pure soul God may at any time manifest himself in whatsoever manner he may choose.

The Christian mystical life is one of great moral and spiritual richness. It has been, and is still, lived by many holy souls, some of them known to others, but the majority, it may be, as hidden as was the Mother of God. This must therefore be for us the true and fullest expression of mysticism, and we may use this as our "control" in all surveys of other types and examples of mystical experience. Its keynote is love and the abandonment of self-love, and the surest sign of its presence is the resolute choice of the unseen rather than the seen, the supernatural rather than the natural, and the growing perception of God, the object of faith and love, as a Being within the soul, absorbing, controlling, directing it, "and there is no reason for marvelling that God should grant such high and rare favours to those souls on whom He bestows good things. For if we consider that He is God, and that He bestows them as God, with infinite love and goodness, it will not seem to us unreasonable. For God said that the Father, the Son and the Holy Spirit would come to him that loved Him and make Their abode in him, and this would come to pass by His making him live and dwell in the Father, the Son and the Holy Spirit, in the life of God".[1]

[1] *Living Flame*, Prologue, first redaction (Peers, III 14).

SELECT BIBLIOGRAPHY

Works on mysticism in all its aspects and meanings are legion, and a wide selection of them will be found in any good encyclopedia. The list below is confined to a few works on traditional Christian and Catholic mysticism as it is understood in the present book.

In this series: DAUJAT, Jean: *Prayer,* and *The Theology of Grace;* ZAEHNER, R. C.: *Christianity and Other Religions* (English edn, *The Catholic Church and World Religions*).

BAKER, Augustine, O.S.B.: *Holy Wisdom,* edited by G. Sitwell, London, Burns and Oates, 1964.

BUTLER, E. C., O.S.B.: *Western Mysticism,* London, Constable, 1922; 2nd edn, expanded, 1928; New York, Harper, 1965.*

Cloud of Unknowing, The: ed. J. McCann, London, Burns and Oates, 1924; revised edn 1952.

DICKEN, E. W. Trueman: *The Crucible of Love: A Study of the Mysticism of St Teresa of Jesus and St John of the Cross,* London, Darton, Longman and Todd, and New York, Sheed and Ward, 1963.

GARRIGOU-LAGRANGE, R., O.P.: *Christian Perfection and Contemplation,* St Louis, Herder, 1946.

HILTON, Walter: *The Scale of Perfection,* ed. G. Sitwell, London, Burns and Oates, 1953.

JOHN OF THE CROSS, ST: *The Complete Works,* ed. and translated by E. A. Peers, 3 vols., London, Burns and Oates, 1934–5; 3 vols. in one, 1964; Westminster, Md, Newman Press, 1953.

KNOWLES, D.: *The English Mystics,* London, Burns and Oates, and New York, Harper, 1961; London, 1964*; New York, 1965.*

PEERS, E. A.: *Spirit of Flame, A Study of St John of the Cross,* London, S.C.M. Press, 1943, and Naperville, Ill., Allenson, 1961. (The best short study.)

PHILIPON, M. M., O.P.: *The Spiritual Doctrine of Sister Elizabeth of the Trinity,* trans. by a Benedictine of Stanbrook, Cork, Mercier Press, and Westminster, Md, Newman Bookshop, 1947.

TERESA OF AVILA, ST: *The Life, by herself*, translated by David Lewis, London, Burns and Oates, 1962. *The Complete Works*, 3 vols., trans. by E. A. Peers, London, Sheed and Ward, 1946.

ZAEHNER, R. C.: *Hindu and Muslim Mysticism*, London, Athlone Press, and New York, Oxford Univ. Press, 1960.

Paperbacks are marked with an asterisk.

Translations of *The Cloud of Unknowing* and St Teresa are in Penguin Books.